Jaws:
The Tom Forsyth Story

Tom Forsyth

Fort Publishing Ltd

First published in 2010 by Fort Publishing Ltd, Old Belmont House,
12 Robsland Avenue, Ayr, KA7 2RW

Graphics by Mark Blackadder

Typeset by 3btype.com

Printed by Bell & Bain Ltd, Glasgow

ISBN: 978-1-905769-20-9

For my wife, Linda, and my family

Contents

Foreword: by Tommy McLean

I am delighted to have the opportunity of writing a foreword for Tom's autobiography. He was a great colleague of mine, firstly at Ibrox and then as assistant manager at both Morton and Motherwell. He is one of those guys who gives everything to the job in hand, someone who never lets you down when the going gets tough.

I knew of Tom from an early age. We were both Lanarkshire lads, him from Stonehouse and me from Ashgill, just a few short miles apart. However, it was when he moved to Rangers in 1972 that I really got to know him well. We would drive in together for training and it was during those journeys that our friendship developed. Later, we would have another passenger for the morning commute: the late, great Davie Cooper, who became a close friend to us both.

When Jock Wallace signed Tom it wasn't what you might call a spectacular signing, but there is no doubt that it developed into a great signing. Tom was exceptional for Rangers. He gave 100 per cent in every single game he played. I put him in the same category as guys like Willie Woodburn, Bobby Shearer, John Brown and of course John Greig. These were players who had an enormous will to win, players who would have run through a brick wall for the club. Like them big Tam was a 'jersey' player; it meant so much to pull on that famous light-blue strip.

The Rangers supporters recognised his worth. They love players who give their all for the cause and no one could have given more. Nor did he do his cause any harm with the fans when he scored the winner in the centenary cup final against Celtic in 1973. I think the Scotland fans will feel the same way. Who could forget the famous challenge he put in on Mick Channon in the closing stages of the 1976 clash with England at Hampden Park? I don't think any other defender in Britain could have made that tackle. It ensured a Scotland win and of course the home-international championship for the first time in years.

Tom Forsyth is often referred to as a hard man or given nicknames like Iron Man or Jaws. And yes it is true that he was a great tackler and ball-winner. I don't think Rangers would have been so successful if he hadn't displayed those qualities week in, week out. Yet there was much more to his game than that. He could also play a bit. Tom was often deployed in midfield at Motherwell and sometimes at Ibrox too. His distribution was excellent and he made a fair amount of goals with runs into the opposition half of the field.

When the time came for us to hang up our boots we both realised that we wanted to stay in the game. In 1983 an opportunity came up for me to take over as manager of Morton, who were then in the first division, and I had no hesitation in asking the Big Man to come with me as my assistant manager. We did pretty well, winning promotion back to the premier league at the first time of asking. Thanks to our successful campaign at Cappielow, we got the chance to take the managerial reins at Fir Park.

There was a big job to be done at Motherwell. The club had just been relegated and for financial reasons was under real pressure to bounce straight back to the premier league. Failure would have hit us hard and perhaps forced us to let go many of the promising young players at the club, players that the club sold for big money further down the line. I was glad to have Tom at my side. He got stuck in, coaching the full timers during the day and then coming back in the evenings to do the same for the part-time players. Not once did he complain about the long hours.

The hard work paid off. For the second season in a row Tom and I guided a club back to the premier league. From then on, Motherwell made steady progress, culminating in the historic Scottish Cup win in 1991 and a third-place finish in the premier league in 1993/94. Tom was an excellent coach, concentrating more on the defensive side while I tended to look after the midfield and attack. It was a great partnership and I think what we achieved speaks for itself.

Money was always tight at Fir Park. We looked after the pennies and that was evident even at training. We used to go to a place called Smithycroft in Hamilton and took twenty balls in a big bag with us. And believe me if we took twenty balls the rule was we came back with twenty balls. But this day, after a training session that Tom felt hadn't gone particularly well, there were only nineteen balls in the bag. It was fairly chucking it down but there was no way Big Tam, perhaps mindful of their performance at training, was going to let those guys off the hook. He had them hunting high and low for that missing ball, making them comb through the long grass in the pouring rain. But it was nowhere to be seen.

Then one of the younger players thought he had the solution.

'Have you counted the ball under your arm?' the bright spark asked Tom.

Sure enough it was ball number twenty.

We had a right good chuckle about that on the drive back to Fir Park.

I count Tom as a true friend, someone who would never let you down. I also count his wife Linda and their three children, Karen, Julie and David, as friends. I wish them well.

Tommy McLean,
Larbert,
September 2010

Acknowledgements

When I was a boy all I wanted to do was play football. I played constantly, first in the street then at schoolboy, amateur and Junior level. There are many people I need to thank, people who gave freely of their time to organise games and to train us. It is people like that who keep grassroots football going and all of us who love the game are in their debt. I had a great career in football and their help and support were invaluable as I moved through the grades. I will never forget those early days in Stonehouse and I would like to take this opportunity to thank each and every one of them.

One of my first influences was the late Roy Douglas, the trainer of Stonehouse Amateurs. Roy was a tough disciplinarian but he had the respect of his players. He would later get me a trial with Birkenshaw Amateurs.

The late Archie Binnie ran Glenavon Amateurs and in fact he signed me for the team. He had willing helpers in his two sons, Douglas and John.

Thanks also to the following people, all of whom played a part in my football career at Stonehouse Amateurs: Jack Bunch, who was club chairman, Ian Murray, secretary, Alex Brown, treasurer, and Walter Rowan, vice chairman.

My father-in-law, Tom Barr, was of course the president of my Junior team, Stonehouse Violet, and he was always on hand to dispense sound career advice and, when the time came, to help me in negotiations with the senior clubs I played for. I greatly appreciate all that he did for me.

Bowls is my other sport. I have been a member of Stonehouse bowling club for decades and I am grateful to everyone there for all the great times I have enjoyed.

I must of course also mention my family. While I was working at George Wilson's in Stonehouse another great chapter in my life began. It was there that I met my future wife, Linda Barr. We fell in love, got married and had three wonderful children, Karen, Julie and David. They in turn have blessed us with five adorable grandchildren, Sophie, Emma, Mason, Cameron and Max. I am affectionately known to them as 'grumpy grampa'.

Tom Forsyth,
Stonehouse
September 2010

1

Early Days

Although I have lived in Stonehouse for as long as I can remember I was actually born a 'Buddie', the nickname given to people from Paisley, Scotland's biggest town. It was January 1949 and my parents – dad David and Mum Anne – were living at 28 Caplethill Road. For some reason my mother decided on a home birth and so it was that on the twenty-third of that month I made my entrance into the world. When my sister Margaret went to bed that night she had a new little brother. Imagine her surprise then when she got up the next day and discovered that she had not one brother but two. While she had been asleep my twin brother, Robert, had arrived.

My parents both had strong links to the land and to farming, something that in the fullness of time would rub off on me too. In those days my father worked at Paisley market, which was then a bustling, lively place devoted to the sale of sheep and cattle from the surrounding farms. My mother's family owned a farm – Cotcastle near Stonehouse – where my maternal grandfather bred, among other livestock, Clydesdale horses. That's how mum and dad got to know each other. Dad had taken a Clydesdale to Cotcastle for breeding and during his visit he met mum. With the family now complete after the birth of twins, mum and dad didn't stay long in Paisley. We moved to Thornlie Park farm and then, when I was two, mum felt that she wanted to be closer to her family and so we moved to Stonehouse, where dad got a job as a machine-man at George Wilson's. I have lived there ever since.

Stonehouse, which has a population of about three thousand, is a down-to-earth, working-class community with no airs and graces. In the nineteenth century it became a major weaving centre, specialising in the production of high-quality silk goods. Many of the terraced cottages occupied by the weavers are still in existence today and have been turned into comfortable family homes. In the latter part of the century, when the weaving industry went into decline, Stonehouse's population turned to the mines and hundreds of men made a living in two pits that were situated just outside the town: Canderrig and Broomfield. Those unable to get a job down the pit looked to agriculture. The people of Stonehouse worked long hours, doing hard physical labour, to earn a living but were proud to do so. There has always been a great community spirit in the town, something that is remarked upon by the town's historian, John R. Young, in his book *Wha's Like Us?* They are just good, honest folk who give of their best.

Dad worked really hard and when he wasn't at work he would be tending the garden, growing a range of vegetable and flowers, of which chrysanthemums were his particular favourites. My Uncle Tam, my father's brother, was a successful nurseryman and he too had a liking for crysanths. It was something that would also rub off on me in the fullness of time. Because dad was so busy we rarely took a holiday and if we did get away it was a day here and a day there. Nothing fancy mind; I remember we often went to a caravan in Craigie Park in Ayr.

Although we certainly weren't wealthy it was a very happy childhood. We lived in a fair-sized terraced house in Angle Street, where Robert and I shared a bedroom, while my sister had her own room. When we were old enough we were sent to Stonehouse primary and then on to Stonehouse secondary. I have to confess I was never keen on the academic side of school. I was a sportsman, enjoying golf, tennis, athletics and, most of all, football.

Robert and I, and all of our pals, would play football morning, noon and night, three-hundred-and-sixty-five days a year. Two, three, four, five a side. Remember, this was the Fifties. There was nothing else to do. No computers, no colour television, no mobile phones, no Play Stations. We played on a pitch on Union Street or if that was being used on waste ground with jackets for goalposts. Often we would just have a kick-about in the street. As there wasn't much traffic in those days it should have been safe. But it didn't stop me almost being killed. I was taking part in yet another impromptu game when I saw my sister Margaret on the other side of the road. Instinctively, I rushed across to see her, without of course looking to see if there was anything coming. There were so few cars then that we just didn't take the precautions that are second nature for children nowadays. But there were buses and as I was crossing the road one almost hit me. Margaret vividly remembers how close that bus came to hitting me and how the driver got out and gave me a right royal row for being so stupid.

I was in the school team at both primary and secondary, as was Robert, who was a good player, and in fact some people thought he was better than me in those days. I played at centre half, in midfield and even as a striker. I always thought there were some promising players at school and I still wonder why they didn't make it in the pro game. It wasn't as if they wouldn't have jumped at the chance of playing for a top club. We all would. If I was pushed for an explanation I just think they lacked what I would call the X factor: call it steel, grit, determination or even sheer bloody-mindedness; it is in the DNA of every top player. As in so many walks of life many are called but few are chosen.

My life in those days revolved around football, whether at school or during my free time. I was the mascot for Stonehouse Thistle Amateurs from the age of nine until I was about twelve. I attended all the home games and would travel right across Scotland with the side.

I hoped through my formative years that I would make it in football. Keen as I was sometimes the challenge seemed insurmountable. Like the day Robert and I went, aged about nine, to a schools cup final at Douglas Park, home to Hamilton Academicals. Stonehouse secondary was playing a team from Uddingston called Viewpark and it was the first game I had ever seen in a proper stadium. Viewpark won easily, by six goals to nil, inspired by their right winger, who, not content with scoring a hat trick, laid on the other three goals for his grateful teammates. It was a virtuoso display by any standards and even at such a tender age I realised just how hard it would be to become a player if that was what I was up against.

Leaving the stadium at the end of the game I heard someone ask: 'Who was that guy on the wing for Viewpark? He was absolutely brilliant.'

'His name is Jimmy Johnstone,' a voice in the crowd replied.

I saw Jinky play many times after that and of course I also played against him for Motherwell and for Rangers. But I have never forgotten that day. Despite being by some distance the smallest guy on the pitch he tore the opposition apart with his control and trickery. Jimmy was just fourteen then but everyone who witnessed his performance could see that he was going right to the top. What a tragedy for Scottish football that we don't produce players like that anymore.

From school football I went to train with Birkenshaw Amateurs in Larkhall, just a few miles from Stonehouse, having been recommended by Roy Douglas, the coach of Stonehouse Amateurs, the team I was mascot for. Birkenshaw had an excellent reputation in youth football and in fact just before I started training there two of their boys – Tommy McLean and Billy Dickson – signed for Kilmarnock. The only problem was that Birkenshaw played at under-sixteen level and I was just a bit on the young side to compete against boys who were two years older. So I moved on again, this time to Glenavon Amateurs, whose home park was in Larkhall. I slotted into their side as an old-fashioned inside forward and managed to notch quite a few goals along the way.

My performances must have caught the eye of the county selectors because I was picked to play for Lanarkshire Select against Scottish Amateurs in, I think, 1965. I was well pleased to be playing at that level but little did I realise that the game would be the most traumatic event of my young life.

I was deployed at right back for Lanarkshire and during an opposition attack I went in for a fifty-fifty ball with their left half, who I later discovered was called Ninian Sommerville. There was a collision which, unfortunately, resulted in Ninian breaking his leg. The crack was so loud it was probably heard in the next county. It was an accident but I felt terrible and the colour drained from my face. As players, coaches and spectators gathered round Ninian I wanted to go over and tell him I was sorry but the nearest person to him was his hulking, muscle-bound teammate, Willie Lynas, someone you would most definitely not want to meet in the proverbial dark alley. Discretion as they say is the better part of valour so I kept my distance as Ninian was eased onto a stretcher and taken off the pitch.

I wasn't in a fit state to play on but our manager, Archie Binnie, said: 'Calm down son. It could have been worse. It could have been you.' I managed to finish the game but it was a close-run thing. There are a couple of interesting postscripts to the story. A couple of weeks later there was a photograph of Ninian Sommerville in the *Daily Record*. It was one of those little human-interest pieces and it showed him, complete with plaster on his broken leg, sitting his school exams. Then a few years later, when I was playing for Stonehouse Violet, who should we sign but Willie Lynas, Ninian's brick shithouse of a teammate. Luckily for me he seemed content to let sleeping dogs lie.

I suppose I was lucky that the only serious injury I was responsible for occurred when I was an unknown. If it had been during my Rangers days, accident or no accident, the media would have had a field day.

We travelled all over with Glenavon, even down to London, where, in 1967, on the eve of the England–Scotland game at Wembley we faced Crystal Palace colts at Selhurst Park. It was a shock to the system when we got into the tunnel and saw our opponents for the first time. They were massive, but that if anything motivated us and we got stuck right in, running out 5–1 winners, with yours truly scoring the opening goal. Our coach was delighted.

The next day we were at Wembley to see Scotland become the first team since the 1966 World Cup to defeat England. My heroes at the time were Jim Baxter and Denis Law and didn't they put on a show. Scotland were superior in every department that afternoon and could have scored a barrow-load if they had pressed home their advantage.[1] But the Scots seemed happier to take the piss out of their opponents, epitomised of course by the gallus Baxter's legendary spot of keepy-uppy and his outrageous flicks. Nevertheless, for a football-mad seventeen-year-old it was an unbelievable experience to see the Scottish

---

[1]   Scotland won 3–2 thanks to goals from Law, Lennox and McCalliog.

fans take over Wembley. And of course I could never have dreamt that ten years later my Scotland teammates and I would write our own little bit of Wembley history.

By the time I went down to Wembley I had also been in the world of work for two years, having left school at the age of fifteen. I was an apprentice joiner with Stonehouse firm, George Wilson. Wilson's was a big concern, with contracts all over Lanarkshire and beyond and had built large chunks of East Kilbride new town. I was assigned to house-building projects in place like Shotts and Bellshill. It was hard graft, rising at first light, working outside in all weathers. But it certainly toughened you up and, one day per week, we got what seemed like a day off when we attended technical college to learn the theory behind the practice. The money I earned as an apprentice joiner hardly put me in the super-tax bracket. I remember the thrill of getting my first wage packet, which contained the princely sum of £3 11s 11d.[2] I also qualified for a share of the tradesman's bonus, which some weeks amounted to all of thirteen shillings. I thought I was a millionaire! I stuck with it, completed my five-year apprenticeship and emerged as a fully time-served joiner, a trade that one day I would have to fall back on.

When time and my football schedule allowed I enjoyed the occasional day out with my pals. I remember one year, I think it was 1966, that I went to Butlin's in Ayr with my two pals, Tam Campbell and Billy Paterson, both of whom were like me about seventeen. After we had sampled the many delights Butlin's had to offer Tam said that he wanted to go on a horse. Reluctantly, I agreed and the three of us mounted up. I have never been more terrified in my life, something that the poor nag must have sensed because it just stood there, refusing to move. Meanwhile, Tam and Billy had enjoyed a great gallop along the beach and when they trotted back to where I was standing they had a right good laugh at my expense. It was the first and last time I ever got on a horse. Incidentally, I must mention Billy's great achievements in

---

[2] Three pounds, eleven shillings and eleven (old) pence – for those of you too young to remember the pre-decimal currency.

Junior football. He played in seven Scottish Junior Cup finals, which must be a record. Four were with Cambuslang Rangers, two with Baillieston and the other was with Stonehouse Violet.

It was also around this time that I got my hands on a winner's medal, although it is not something you would read about in the record books. A pal asked if I would play for a team called Hamilton Young Farmers in the deciding game of a young farmer's tournament. I agreed. So we took on a team from Ayrshire on a pitch that was so wet it resembled a paddy field. In truth the match should have been called off but the farmers took the view that they kicked more water off their wellies on a daily basis and so it was game on. We won easily and I distinguished myself by scoring a hat trick. I picked up my first winner's medal, which was a real thrill despite the fact that the standard of football was not exactly top drawer. My only gripe was that I had to wash myself in a cow's trough after the game and ended up going home caked in mud.

When my own playing commitments allowed I was a regular spectator at the football. Fir Park, being close at hand, was a favourite ground but it wasn't just because the journey time was short. There were some remarkable players at Fir Park in those days and they were known collectively as the Ancell Babes. The Babes were named for manager Bobby Ancell, who signed and developed so much young talent during his time at Motherwell in the late Fifties and early Sixties.

The team was a joy to watch in those years and the list of great players is almost endless. Perhaps the best known is Ian St John, who went on to play for Bill Shankly's all-conquering Liverpool side and of course for Scotland. The Saint was an instinctive striker who scored one of the quickest hat tricks of all time against Hibs in 1959; it took him all of two-and-a-half minutes. Then there was Charlie Aitken, a right half who was superb in the air as well as being strong in the tackle. Charlie was twice voted player of the year and many commentators rated him the best uncapped right half in the country. Pat Quinn was a clever, scheming inside forward who was also deadly from the penalty spot and was capped by Scotland. And what about Willie Hunter, another Scotland cap, and a man who as well as being a regular scorer made so many goals for his colleagues; he was for many observers the most skilful of the Babes. Ancell's philosophy was to attack, attack and attack again and his young charges played some beautiful, flowing football. They would undoubtedly have been contenders for many honours had bigger clubs not come knocking and taken away the likes of St John and Quinn.

I went to Fir Park with my pals, especially Ken Hamilton, who was also a keen street footballer. Ken and I would get taken to games by Tam Miller, who worked with my dad, and Dave Jackson, who was Ken's uncle. When we got to the ground they would head for the stand while we would pay at the boy's gate and go on to the terraces. I always appreciated Tam and Dave taking us with them and years later, after I had moved to Ibrox and out of gratitude for what they had done for me, I left tickets at Hampden for them for a Scottish Cup semi-final between Rangers and Motherwell, which was played in March 1976.

Tam and Dave must have enjoyed the early exchanges because Motherwell at one stage were 2–0 up but helped by a number of decisions that their fans thought were of the dodgy variety – including the award of a penalty to us – Rangers fought back and won the game by three goals to two. That night, well pleased by the result, I went for a pint at the bowling club. Tam Miller came in but, being a keen Motherwell fan, he wouldn't speak to me! He was clearly still sore about the decisions at Hampden, decisions that he thought had cost his team a place in the Scottish Cup final. Tam was so gutted in fact that he didn't speak to me for months.

2

The Wonderful World of Junior Football

Today when pundits write about the Junior game they are often trying to give their readers a laugh. It is caricatured as the country cousin of football, full of hard men knocking lumps out of each other on pitches situated in former mining villages that are not even smooth enough to be described as a ploughed field. That is unfair. There are some excellent players operating in that grade of football and many of them, thanks to successful social clubs and the like, get higher wages than those attached to senior clubs. The elite sides in Scotland, with their youth academies and training complexes, no longer look to the Juniors for talent but the game at that level is vibrant and long may it last.

It hasn't always been this way. The Junior grade has produced great players by the dozen, and I mean *great* players. Take Rangers. Sam English was captured from Yoker Athletic, George Young came to Ibrox from Kirkintilloch Rob Roy and Torry Gillick was a Petershill player when Ranger signed him. If you want more recent examples I could mention Ronnie McKinnon, who played for both Benburb and Dunipace, and Bobby Russell, who joined up from Shettleston. Multiply that by ten, fifteen or even twenty to cover the other leading clubs in Scotland and you will see what I mean.

So I was delighted when my local Junior side, Stonehouse Violet, made me in the youngest player in their history. I was sixteen and I felt that to join a Junior club was a definite step in the right direction. I joined Violet after playing for Stonehouse Thistle under-eighteens. Thistle would later play in the Junior league, taking the place of the Violet.[3] I remember getting a signing-on fee of £10 from my new club – which seemed like a fortune – and promptly splashing most of it on my first suit.

I was with the Violet for less than two years but I learnt so much and my experience there definitely helped me become a better player. I was lucky to have a great coach: George McMillan, whose nickname was 'captain'. George had been a goalkeeper, and a very good one at that. He played for Ipswich Town under Alf Ramsey, as well as for several Scottish clubs, including Stirling Albion and Hamilton Accies. 'Captain' had tremendous experience and a deep love of football and he would tell me about the matches he had played in and the players he had played against. Hearing his stories made me even more determined to make it to the highest levels of the game.

Despite the many good players in the Juniors, conditions were often on the basic side. Our home ground, Tilework Park, was hardly conducive to flowing football and at the edge of the pitch, instead of grass, there was ash. I put in a lot of slide tackles and after games my legs would be cut and covered in blood and dirt due to abrasions from the ash. I always remember our trainer, Tam Finnan, the first time he saw the state of my legs, saying to me:

'Go and clean that. If you don't clean it right I will come in and do it with the wire brush.'

I did my best to get the dirt out with a scrubbing brush but it was always a hard job. Then, the following Saturday, just when my legs were beginning to heal, I would be out there slide tackling for all I was worth and turning my legs to mush yet again.

Given that we relied on part-time players, many of whom were,

---

3   The 'Violet' has a rather chequered history. They came back into the Juniors at a later date only to go under again in 2008. Happily, the club has again risen from the ashes and at the time of writing is now competing in the Juniors.

like me, youngsters, results could be erratic. I vividly recall an away game at Shotts Bon Accord, who had a huge pitch, even bigger than Hampden I believe. We scored first, prompting the father of scorer Eddie Feeney to declare 'That's my boy. That's my boy. He's scored!' Eddie had indeed scored but the problem was that we had annoyed Shotts, who proceeded to use the full width of their pitch to give us a football lesson. They knocked in nine goals without any further reply from us.

The Stonehouse Violet fans were something else. One Saturday we were playing Sauchie, away from home, in the Scottish Junior Cup. Our supporters gathered in the Black Bull, a well-known Stonehouse pub, and after a couple of pints they boarded the bus. The bus managed to go all of a mile before stopping at the Shawlands hotel, which is between Stonehouse and Larkhall, before stopping for more liquid refreshment.[4] You can imagine the state they were in when they finally got to Sauchie. In fact when they arrived one of the guys struck a bizarre bet with one of the home fans. He wagered £5 (and £5 was £5 in those days) that Stonehouse would get the first shy. The problem was that he didn't get a neutral to hold the money and the Sauchie fan promptly got on his toes, leaving our guy considerably out of pocket.

After the game more stops were made as the supporters' bus made its way ever so slowly back to Stonehouse. They called in at Tullibody social club where they got a bit rowdy and were thrown out. At the next port of call – after, oh, the fifteenth round of drinks that day – they made so much noise that the police arrived and promptly arrested a whole squad of our fans. Although they were completely innocent some of the team also got lifted and I will always remember sitting outside the police station at two in the morning waiting for my team-mates to be released from a cell.

I am not quite sure how my game managed to improve given all the shenanigans but improve it did. Senior clubs, who routinely sent scouts to games in the Junior leagues, noticed me and the result was an

---

4   The Shawlands was owned at that time by Celtic legend Bertie Auld. I know Bertie well and we have organised Old Firm golf outings together.

invitation to a trial with Dundee United, which consisted of a single training session during the day. United didn't offer me anything but later I went on trial with Motherwell and after reserve-team coach Willie McSeveney had weighed me up he recommended me to manager Bobby Howitt, who later signed me. As a Lanarkshire lad and a Motherwell fan as a boy I was delighted.

There was interest too from a rather unexpected quarter. After one game Celtic manager Jock Stein asked our club president (and my future father-in-law) Tom Barr, if I was the Thistle player 'who had a twin brother'. Clearly, Stein was aware of me.

'Are you interested in signing him?' Mr Barr asked.

'Not when our neighbours on the other side of the city are looking at him.'

In one fell swoop our president had discovered that both sides of the Old Firm had been keeping a weather eye on me. Rangers would have been a dream come true but people often ask me if I would have signed for Celtic. With apologies to Rangers fans everywhere I am afraid the answer is yes. Let's be honest: what football-mad youngster in Scotland would have turned down a man like Jock Stein?

Actually, I thought I had lost my chance with Motherwell after Bobby Howitt came to watch me after being given the nod by his scouts. He was at our match with Shotts Bon Accord. It was a hard, hard game – entirely typical of the Junior football we all know and love. Their centre forward had been giving me grief right through the match and so, with twenty minutes to go, I got in a bit of retribution. The ref judged that my tackle was illegal and promptly sent me for an early bath. I knew Bobby was there watching me, along with his chief scout, and I immediately regretted the rash challenge.

'I hope that hasn't ruined his chances,' Tom Barr said to Howitt after the game.

'No way,' the Motherwell supremo replied. 'I like guys with fire in their belly.'

Three months later Bobby Howitt signed me for Motherwell.

3

Motherwell: Making the Grade

I was a raw eighteen-year-old kid when I made the step-up to senior football in the summer of 1967. Signing for Motherwell was a huge thrill. I had always of course been a fan and had regularly attended their home games. I signed a contract on part-time terms, combining football with my apprenticeship as a joiner. It meant that financially I had never had it so good. Although I didn't get a signing-on fee from Motherwell my wage was £19 per week – plus a bonus of £10 if I was in the first-team pool and we happened to win on the Saturday. If you added that to the earnings from my day job it amounted to a tidy sum for a teenager.

When I joined the club was in its accustomed place in the top tier of Scottish football, the old first division, but although we had a number of highly talented players the cracks were beginning to show. It was very much a transitional season. Some of the Ancell Babes – for example John Martis and Andy Weir – were still at the club but coming to the end of their careers. At the same time new players were being drafted into the side: Dixie Deans and Davie Whiteford were recent arrivals and were beginning to make a real impact. In the twelve months after I signed guys like John Goldthorpe, Joe Wark, Tom Donnelly and Jumbo Muir would also be recruited.

In the meantime the team floundered. In fact 1967/68, my first season at Fir Park, was a shocker. Motherwell finished second bottom of the league, a long way behind the team in third-bottom spot, and we were relegated to the second division. We had only managed six wins all season, and somehow contrived to lose twenty-one of the thirty-four league games. The only personal consolation was that I made my first-team debut – coming on as a sub – against Stirling Albion on 14 October 1967 and then got my first start against Aberdeen the following month. I fact I managed to start in twelve consecutive games after the Aberdeen match before dropping once again to the bench.

It wasn't all plain sailing as a part-timer. I trained two nights a week, on Tuesdays and Thursdays, after finishing work at Wilson's. I say trained but for most of the time we were restricted to running round the park or to workouts in the gym, which seemed to be the game plan for the part-timers. Much to our annoyance we never actually saw a ball. When we were eventually given one I didn't know whether to eat it, kick it or stick it up my arse! Even when I got to play in practice matches – for the reserves against the first team, a source of great excitement for a youngster – you were expected to know your place in the pecking order. I remember one day I was up against the legendary John Martis, who was then still a first-team regular but inevitably was slowing up. I was playing at inside forward and latched on to a through ball. With the confidence of youth I outpaced Mr Martis and rifled the ball into the net. Pleased as punch with my goal I turned away and began to jog back to our half for the restart. But John was not a happy camper.

'What's your fucking game?' the great man roared.

It was then I realised that I should have saved John's blushes and ballooned the ball over the bar.

I would get dropped off at Fir Park for training by the George Wilson workers' bus, which meant I was often there earlier than my teammates. I recall this particular day when I walked in that the dressing room was empty and in complete darkness.

The phone rang. I picked up the receiver.

'Who's that?' a voice I recognised as Bobby Howitt's asked.

'It's Tom Forsyth.'

'You're playing in a reserve game at Celtic Park tonight,' he barked.

'But I'm still in my working clothes, jeans and a donkey jacket,' I protested. 'And I've had nothing to eat.'

'Just go and get a sandwich at the Fir Park cafe.'

Twenty minutes later I was on the team bus to the east end of Glasgow. I can't tell you how embarrassed and uncomfortable I was. Turning up at the home of the European champions in a donkey jacket and workman's jeans is just not the done thing. To rub salt into the wound I was concussed during the game after colliding with Celtic striker Joe McBride, who had been one of my idols when he played for the 'Well. There were no hard feelings and nowadays Joe and I often have a beer together when we take part in charity golf tournaments.

Some people might think that rookies like me would have been cut a little slack by older, more experienced players. Not a chance; at least not in those days. Show the slightest weakness and someone was sure to rub your nose in it. I remember playing in another reserve game against Celtic and Stevie Chalmers and I running for a ball that had been lobbed through the centre of our defence. I managed to get there first and tried a delicate lob to our keeper. But I misjudged it and the ball flew over the goalie's head and into the net.

As I lay on the ground, disconsolate, Chalmers walked past me, patted my head and remarked:

'Well done son.'

I was seething at Stevie's reaction to my mistake. But I got my own back. We beat them by two goals to one.

I seem to have had a few run-ins with Celtic, or future Celtic, players in those days. I remember coming up against the highly talented Harry Hood in the days when he played for Clyde. Before the game Bobby Howitt, recognising Hood as a real threat, gave me just two words of advice: 'mark Hood'. And so I did, sticking like a limpet to him for the entire ninety minutes. In fact I must have made a great impression on Harry, because when we were shaking hands at the end of the game he said, in a rather weary tone of voice: 'Are you no' coming home for your tea son?'

You also had to be up for the physical challenge because there were some right tough places and some right tough characters in that era. I had to grow up quickly let me tell you. One of the hardest opponents I came up against was Billy 'Sugar' Osborne, a centre forward with Morton who was built like a Sherman tank. We had some great tussles and coping with physical challenges from the likes of Sugar really toughened me up. It wasn't just Morton's forwards I had to worry about. In one game at Fir Park, we were up I think by a single goal and Morton were chasing the game. That prompted them to put centre half Stan Rankin up front to help their forwards in the search for an equaliser. When a long ball was launched from the back I went up to head it clear. The next thing I remember was waking up in the old Law hospital, near Wishaw. It was only then that I found out what had happened. According to my teammates, when I was in the air, Stan had back-headed me, breaking my nose and leaving my face black and blue for months to come.

But for me Airdrie's quaint little Broomfield stadium was by far the worst. The Ne'erday derby – with both sets of fans fired up and Lanarkshire bragging rights at stake – was particularly tense. We went there on the first of January 1968 and it is a game I will never forget.

In the first place it should never have been played. It was bitterly cold and the ground was brick hard. But I think that the committee that ran Airdrie wanted the extra revenue that playing on New Year's Day brought and so play we did. Broomfield was, as I have said, a quaint little ground and when you left the dressing room you walked through a stand behind the goals at the Airdrie end and out onto on the park. The abuse we got from the home fans was something else; these guys had A levels in intimidation.

I went onto that park with the rather naive assumption that I would be able to play some tidy football, maybe spray a few nice passes around. I reckoned without Messrs Davie Marshall and Willie McPheat, two of the toughest men I have ever come up against. I was dilly-dallying in the centre of midfield, looking to make the perfect pass, when I was hit by a steam train. It was Mr Marshall, showing the world what he thought of some smart kid showboating on his manor. Then, later in the game, when I slipped on the icy surface and landed on my arse, his partner-in-crime Mr McPheat walked right over the top of me with his big, tackety boots (at least they felt tackety to me). I got a real education that day.

But there were never any grudges borne. That was the way things were then. You played hard, neither asking for nor receiving any quarter and then at the end of the game it was handshakes all round. I am still friendly with many of the guys I played against and in the mid 1990s I bumped into Davie Marshall at Gleneagles during the Scottish Professional Golfers championship. My mate and I were watching the players practise on the putting green when a face I will never forget hove into view. It was Davie.[5]

'Do you not know me?' he asked.

'Know you Davie? I waken up through the night in a cold sweat dreaming about you.'

* * *

My busy life meant there were few opportunities for socialising although I did find the time to fall in love and get married. My future wife – then Linda Barr – also worked at George Wilson's. She was the daughter of Mr Thomas Barr, who was of course the president of Stonehouse Violet when I was a player there. One day Linda was being given a lift to work by her dad when she spotted me on the pavement.

'Who's that?' she asked her father.

Her dad peeped his horn, gave me a wave and told her my name. He also told her that I played for his team, the Violet, which meant nothing to Linda as she didn't have the slightest interest in football, a game about which, even after all the years married to a professional, she is still completely indifferent.

Slowly but surely we got to know each other. I ran the works sweep and would often go into the offices to sell her and the other admin staff a ticket. It actually took us two years to get together after the 'peeping of the horn' but we finally became a couple after a dance in the welfare institute in Stonehouse. We would meet in a pub in Hamilton on a Saturday night after a game and it always used to annoy her that I would insist on reading the 'Pink' edition of the *Evening Times* or the *Evening Citizen* to catch up with what had happened elsewhere in the world of Scottish football. I am afraid her attempts

---

5   Sadly, Davie passed away a few years ago.

at conversation were met with a grunt until I had finished reading the papers.

After going steady for a couple of years I popped the question when we were out for a drive in the country and we got married on 17 June 1971, which was of course well into the close season. We wanted a church wedding and the service was held in the United Free Church in Stonehouse, where Linda is now an elder, and where, I am pleased to say, our three children were baptised. I still go to church occasionally, but not as much as Linda would like.

Next year we will celebrate our fortieth wedding anniversary and I will always be grateful for all the help and support she has given me over the years. I know it couldn't have been easy for her when I was playing, what with three young children to look after and me often away on tour with Rangers or Scotland. But she coped admirably and without a word of complaint, a tribute to the way she was brought up and her strength of character.

4

Motherwell: Back to the Big Time

After playing the likes of Rangers and Celtic – then two of Europe's most powerful sides – not to mention excellent teams like Aberdeen, Hibs and Dundee United the thought of going to smaller grounds like Cliftonhill and Shielfield, home to Albion Rovers and Berwick Rangers respectively, was hardly as exciting although we still gave anyone we faced total respect.[6] There was only one way to put right the disastrous relegation season of 1967/68 and that was to bounce back to the first division at the first time of asking.

We did it. And we did it in style. In fact, spurred on by a fierce determination to get out of the lower league, we walked it, winning the second-division championship by a margin of eleven points. At a time when it was still two points for a win that took some doing. Our record in 68/69 was nothing short of amazing. We lost only two of our thirty-six league games, both away from home, while winning thirty. Our strikers were on fire as we racked up 112 league goals, giving us an average of more than three goals per game. The defence was equally solid, conceding just twenty-three times.

On a personal level it was also a very rewarding season. I was now

---

6   There were only two senior leagues in Scotland in those days, a first division of eighteen clubs and a second division of twenty.

a regular in the first team, where I was deployed on the right side of midfield. If anything I would say that I was something of an attacking midfielder and in that role I weighed in with fifteen goals, two of them in the League Cup. I even got three doubles in the league, two of them in successive matches. Despite the fact that I would later come to prominence as a centre back – my preferred position – I felt comfortable in the midfield and would have been happy to continue in that area of the side if it meant I was getting a regular start.

It was just one of those campaigns in which every player in the team was at the top of his game. Davie Whiteford was a real stalwart at right back and a reliable penalty taker to boot. His partner, Joe Wark, was a real find at left back, having just made the step up from Junior outfit Irvine Meadow. Tom Donnelly (the father of the future Celtic player, Simon) and Willie McCallum were a formidable partnership in the centre of defence while Peter McCloy or Keith MacRae were their usual dependable selves in goal.

The midfield proved to be a solid unit with Jimmy Wilson, Billy Campbell and I all making a good contribution. Up front we had Jackie McInally (also the father of a future Celtic star, in this case Alan, who would go on to play for Aston Villa and Bayern Munich) who knocked in his fair share of goals. Jackie played alongside the man who was without doubt our talisman: John 'Dixie' Deans.

Dixie was a one-off. And I mean a one-off. He kept us all going in the dressing room with his stories, his endless practical jokes and his sheer charisma. I think every club needs a character like that to get his teammates buzzing. He was a cavalier, a bit of a rebel; someone thanks to his hot head who was no stranger to the beaks at Park Gardens, headquarters of the Scottish Football Association.

But by God he could play.

Deans was an instinctive goal scorer. He always seemed to be in the right place at the right time. I would put him in the same mould as an Ally McCoist or a Frank McAvennie; a true penalty-box predator. He got thirty goals that season, a haul that included two hat tricks and five doubles. The only blot on his copybook was being sent off in the Ne'er-day derby against Hamilton after a 'handbags' scuffle with their keeper. But that's Dixie for you; there's never a dull moment when he's around.

That season was epitomised by the day at Fir Park on which we clinched the league-championship flag. It was 14 April 1969 and we sent out the following team to face Stenhousemuir.

MacRae, Whiteford, Wark, Forsyth, McCallum, Campbell, Muir, Donnelly, Deans, Wilson, Goldthorpe

We ran riot from the get-go. I made the first goal, which came after just two minutes. I floated a long ball through the centre of their defence and Dixie, as he had done all season, was onto it in a flash. As their keeper came out he showed all the confidence of a man in peak form by whipping it into the corner of the net. We needed four to reach our century of goals for the season and by the interval we had reached that milestone thanks to counters from Goldthorpe, Muir and Donnelly. In the second half we relaxed and played some beautiful football, running out winners by seven goals to one. I felt a bit sorry for Stenhousemuir but they were gracious in defeat despite the score-line and applauded us from the field at time up.

We were back in the big time at the first attempt.

It was a feather in the cap of manager Bobby Howitt. He had been under pressure following our relegation from the top flight but had now got himself back in the good books of our fans. For my money he was a good manager; a quiet guy who went about his business without much fuss.

How would I compare him to the other managers I have worked with?

He certainly wasn't charismatic, like Jock Wallace, or flamboyant like Ally MacLeod, nor even a great tactician like Tommy McLean. Maybe that is why his Motherwell teams never hit the heights. His best league finish in the top flight was eighth; not bad but not exactly earth-shattering. That said he did preside over some very strong performances in the cup competitions.

* * *

We always looked forward to cup games in those days. They seemed to bring out the best in us and if we never quite made the break-through and reached a final we gave the fans plenty of excitement along the way.

In 1969/70 we raced through our League Cup section unbeaten to set up a quarter-final encounter with Morton. It was a home-and-away affair and we travelled to Cappielow for the first leg, which was played on 10 September 1969. Despite going into the game full of confidence after great early-season form we got a real doing, courtesy of two goals from Morton's star striker, and future Scotland cap, Joe Harper, and an own goal from Willie McCallum.

Facing a 3–0 deficit most pundits – and to be fair most Motherwell fans – thought we were down and out. But two weeks later, at a packed Fir Park, we showed our true colours. People who were there tell me it was the most exciting game they had seen at the old ground for years.

We ripped into Morton right from the kick off, peppering their goal with shots from every angle. I particularly remember a blistering thirty-yard effort from Dixie Deans that forced a wonderful save from their keeper. Then, after twenty-five minutes, we made the break-through. From a set piece the ball fell to Jackie McInally in the box and he blasted it into the roof of the net. Our fans went crazy; I had never heard noise like it at Fir Park.

We kept up the onslaught in the second half but were again frustrated by their goalie, Denmark international Lief Nielsen, who played a real blinder that night. It was going to need a bit of magic and sure enough we managed to produce one. It started with Dixie. After a brilliant turn he sent Joe Wark rampaging down the left flank with a precision pass. Joe crossed for Jim Muir, who coolly controlled the ball and picked his spot. The momentum was now most definitely with us and with sixteen minutes to go I managed to latch onto a loose ball inside the box and slotted home the aggregate equaliser.

Two things have stayed with me from that night. Nielsen's performance, which was close to world class and kept them in the tie, and the backing we got from the terracing. You will have heard the saying 'calm down to a frenzy'; that is a good description of the Motherwell fans during the game. We couldn't have done it without them.

The tie was now 3–3 on aggregate but instead of extra time there was a play-off at Ibrox, which we won 1–0 to set up a semi-final at Hampden with St Johnstone. Once again we went into the game brimming with confidence. After all just a few weeks before the semi we had beaten them comfortably by four goals to one. Sadly we bombed, turning in probably our worst performance of the season as they scored twice without reply to set up a meeting with Celtic in the final.

I don't think I have ever felt so low after a game and I was still feeling sorry for myself when I turned up for training the next night. I wasn't looking forward to going in to Fir Park and I hoped the coaching staff might take pity on us and make it a nice, easy session with a bit of ball work and maybe a five-a-side match to finish things off. Not a bit of it. The coach, Wilson Humphries, himself a former Motherwell player, had clearly not been impressed by our efforts and as a punishment he made us run round the pitch for the entire two hours. That really pissed me off. We had given our all against the Saints but had played poorly. These things happen to every team, perhaps due to nerves or a temporary loss of form, and I felt Wilson was well out of order. Most of us had day jobs and to come in after a shift, not to mention a hard game the night before, and be expected to run for miles round a track was a punishment too far.

We also put in some creditable performances in the Scottish Cup. In the same season that we got to the League Cup semi-final we had good wins over St Johnstone and Inverness Caledonian (then in the Highland League) and were drawn to play Kilmarnock at Rugby Park in the quarter-final. Roared on by a crowd of 16,574 it was a game we should have won but it was the old story of missed chances and great saves from the opposition keeper. Then, inevitably, and completely against the run of play, up popped (Motherwell-born) Ross Mathie to power home a header and put Killie through to the semis.

Our other run to the quarter-finals of the Scottish Cup came in 1971/72 and was memorable for a number of reasons – and not just football ones. In the third round we comfortably disposed of Montrose and when our name came out of the hat for the next round we found ourselves up against Ayr United at Somerset Park. Ayr were then a top-flight club like us and, led by their irrepressible manager Ally MacLeod, they were particularly formidable at home. It was a tough, somewhat bad-tempered game in which defences were most definitely on top and it ended goalless.

The replay was scheduled for the following Wednesday but the problem was that the country was gripped by industrial chaos and a miners' strike. We were in the middle of a three-day week and compulsory power cuts and not even football clubs were exempt. The upshot was that we couldn't use our floodlights and so kick-off was scheduled for three o' clock. The fact that the game was taking place when most of our fans were meant to be at work didn't seem to have much effect on the attendance as 11,648 rolled up to watch an excellent cup tie. Ayr took the lead through their very own 'Dixie', centre forward Alex Ingram – who would become one of my most formidable opponents – but we won through thanks to goals from Brian Heron and Kirkie Lawson.

That set the scene for the most eagerly anticipated game of my five years at Fir Park: a home Scottish Cup quarter-final against Rangers. The demand to see the game was phenomenal, with hundreds of angry fans being turned away by police when a limited number of stand tickets went on sale to the general public. There was a huge row about the alleged unfair distribution of briefs with the story even making the front page of the *Motherwell Times* on 17 March 1972, under the headline 'Big Game Ticket Row Rocks Fir Park'.

Somehow 28,500 fans managed to squeeze their way into the ground and they were rewarded with a pulsating game of football. We managed to come back from an early Rangers goal to lead 2–1 and it looked as if we would be going through to the semi-final until Colin Stein popped up to equalise with only seventeen minutes remaining. It was a shattering blow as I felt we had more than matched Rangers and I also believed we had been denied a clear penalty when Bomber Jackson fouled Jim McCabe inside the box. I have often wondered if that game put me on the Ibrox radar as I thought I had played quite well. The old adage that you only get one chance against the Old Firm was once again proved true and in the replay at Ibrox we put in a battling performance but went down by four goals to two.

5

David Against Goliath: Motherwell in the Texaco Cup

When I look back on those years at Fir Park I take the view that the games we played in the Texaco Cup in 1970/71 represented the high-water mark of my time there. We took on two top quality sides from the elite of English football and were not found wanting. The Texaco Cup was designed for teams in England and Scotland that had not finished high enough in their domestic leagues to qualify for Europe.[7] First up was Stoke City, whose star man was goalkeeper Gordon Banks, a World Cup winner under Sir Alf Ramsay in 1966. But the men from the Potteries had very capable players throughout the side: guys like Jimmy Greenhoff, who was later sold to Manchester United for a big fee; England international Mike Pejic; John Mahoney, who won more than fifty caps for Wales; Dennis Smith, one of their greatest-ever players and a man who would make a big name for himself in management when he hung up his boots.

Gordon Banks showed precisely why Ramsey had so much faith in his ability during that first leg at Fir Park. He pulled off a string of

---

[7] The competition, which initially included teams from Ireland, ran for five seasons from 1970/71 until 1974/75, at which point Texaco withdrew sponsorship.

world-class saves as we hit them with wave after wave of attack. I will never forget two of the saves: the first came when he somehow got a fist to the ball after Jackie McInally connected with a Dixie Deans cross; the second was no less miraculous as he dived full stretch to turn a thunderous Deans shot around the post. We did manage to breach his defences when John Goldthorpe slammed the ball home for the only goal of the game, but I reckon Banks saved his team from a real doing that night. For my part I was pleased with my own performance against such a high-calibre outfit. The fact is I looked forward to games of that stature and didn't seem to suffer any nerves at the prospect of facing top opposition.

If the first leg had been dominated by the performance of a keeper the second leg at the Victoria Ground on 30 September 1970 was no different. But this time it was our custodian, Keith MacRae, who took the plaudits. They were clearly stung by the defeat in the first leg and took the game to us right from kick-off. Keith was magnificent. Stoke would have buried us in the first twenty minutes but for a succession of brilliant saves from the big man. We gradually inched our way into the game and with half an hour on the clock we took a shock lead through Jackie McInally. Teams often get frustrated when they are so much on top and then lose a goal and Stoke, who had a fantastic home record against the top English sides, were no exception. A bit of a roughhouse ensued for the next fifteen minutes in which their players put in some meaty challenges and we responded in kind. No one was booked despite kicks and punches being thrown; no one that is until yours truly got his name taken for a foul on Greenhoff. I didn't think it merited a booking but the referee had clearly reached the end of his tether and had to make an example of someone.

Stoke grabbed an equaliser after forty-one minutes and then came out all guns blazing after the interval. They managed to take the lead on the night but despite chances at both ends – with Keith again out-standing – the ninety minutes ended 2–1 in their favour and 2–2 on aggregate. If the away-goals rule had been in operation we would have been through to the next round but now we were faced with thirty minutes of extra time, which, to be fair, the home side almost completely dominated. Neither team managed to score in extra time so the tie would now be settled by a penalty shoot-out. I didn't take one and although we missed two of our five, Keith managed to save two of their efforts.

It was sudden death and the focus was now even more firmly on Keith. He didn't let us down, making a great save from Stoke's sixth spot kick. It meant that if John Goldthorpe could hold his nerve and put the ball away we were through. And hold his nerve he did, coolly ramming the ball home as if it was a practice match.

The scenes at the end of the shoot-out were incredible. Our fans, who had also been put through an emotional wringer, invaded the park to hail our victory while we carried Keith off shoulder high in recognition of what he had done that night. He had more than matched the performance of Gordon Banks at Fir Park; not bad for a nineteen-year-old. Elsewhere in this book I pick Peter McCloy for my Motherwell select but Keith ran him a close second and I wasn't in the least bit surprised when he became the most expensive goalkeeper in the world after being transferred to Manchester City in 1973 for £100,000. Bobby Howitt was ecstatic, the result all the more sweet given that he had played for Stoke for a number of years.

If we thought beating Stoke had been a big ask our opponents in the next round were even more formidable. We were drawn to face Tottenham Hotspur, then as now one of the biggest clubs in the world.

Managed by the legendary Bill Nicholson – the first man to win the coveted league and FA Cup double in the modern era – Spurs had genuine class throughout their team, in many instances world class. The only surprise was that they had failed to qualify for Europe, but that was a failure they would put right that season by qualifying for the UEFA Cup and then going on to win the trophy in 1972. When you looked at the players at Nicholson's disposal it is little wonder they were so successful.

Their last line of defence was Pat Jennings, the man with the biggest hands in football, and one of the best keepers on the planet. In central defence there was Mike England, a real colossus, who, despite his surname, was a Wales international. Cyril Knowles at left back was a formidable operator: a wonderful crosser of the ball, an England international and the inspiration for the chart hit 'Nice One, Cyril'. In midfield Spurs were no less formidable with England internationals Alan Mullery and Martin Peters (a World Cup winner in '66) providing the ammunition for the front men and weighing in with their fair share of goals. The two strikers – England international and Tottenham's record signing Martin Chivers and Scotland legend Alan Gilzean – were right out of the top drawer. Chivers was a big, powerful man and a prolific marksman for both club and country, while Gilzean had been a member of Dundee's championship-winning side of 1962 and had been sold to Spurs for £72,500, a huge sum for the early Sixties. Despite this formidable array of talent it was one of their lesser lights that caused us most trouble over the two legs: left winger Jimmy Pearce.

With a line up like that it is hardly surprising that few pundits, or Motherwell fans, fancied us to progress to the semi-final. Our task was made even harder because Spurs were in a rich vein of form: third in the first division and unbeaten in ten games. On paper we had no chance, so it is just as well that football isn't played on paper.

We travelled to London for the first leg full of anticipation. It doesn't get much bigger for a team like Motherwell than playing Tottenham Hotspur in a stadium like White Hart Lane. Throughout my career I have always relished the big occasion; I didn't seem to suffer from stage fright at that level and I like to think that the bigger the occasion the better I performed. I now had another chance to put that theory to the test.

Despite all of our grand designs the first half was almost a disaster. I say almost a disaster because we managed to get in at half time with just a two-goal deficit when in all honesty if they had taken their chances the tie would have been dead and buried. With Alan Mullery pulling the strings in midfield and Cyril Knowles and Jimmy Pearce combining to good effect on the left we were on the rack for almost the whole forty-five minutes. Chivers got the first from a wicked Knowles cross and then Martin Peters ghosted in to score with a trademark header seconds before half-time.

It was a different story in the second half. Whether they eased off, or we stopped showing them too much respect, I really don't know but whatever the reason we played out of our skins. This time it was our turn to do the pressing and press we did. Tom Donnelly made it 2–1 eight minutes after the break and, having thrown caution to the wind, we grabbed an equaliser with twenty minutes to go. It must rank as one of the best goals of Jackie McInally's career. Receiving the ball in the box he cleverly turned Mike England and calm as you like sent an unstoppable shot past big Pat Jennings. A draw now seemed the most likely outcome but maybe a bit of complacency crept into our play because we let them back into it. Deep into injury time Knowles again combined with Pearce and sent in a wickedly accurate cross, which Peters bundled home. Before the game I suppose we would readily have accepted a 3–2 defeat but after such a spirited comeback we felt totally deflated.

We now had a fortnight to get over our loss, which wasn't made any easier by a 5–0 home defeat to Celtic in the league on the Saturday before the return leg. That of course was a very poor result but the Texaco Cup was undoubtedly preying on our minds. I said as much to the *Daily Record*, telling them in an interview that, 'We may all have been thinking about the Spurs clash as we were playing Celtic.' Dixie Deans, irrepressible as ever, was in confident mood and was clearly not fazed by the guy who would be marking him, no matter how big his reputation. He boldly announced to the *Record* that:

> I know people are saying Mike England is the best centre half in Britain. But that doesn't worry me. When I played against him at White Hart Lane I didn't find him that difficult to beat. I intend to make him just as disappointed in the result tomorrow night as I was in his play.

Some people would find a statement like that to be unbelievably arrogant. Others might say it was foolish, because it was likely to fire the opposition up. But I don't think Dixie cared. He oozed confidence from every pore and to be honest I think that worked wonders for our morale.

Our fans clearly hadn't stopped believing either and I couldn't believe the sight that greeted me when I ran out with the rest of the team to face our English visitors. There have been bigger Fir Park crowds – I have played in front of them – but to see that many people there on a chilly night in early November under the floodlights was a bit special. The crowd was said to number 22,000 but given the noise they made it seemed more like 42,000. And how they sang and chanted and shouted encouragement, inspired no doubt by the fact that it was English opposition we were facing. Pardon the cliché but the fans really were our twelfth man that night, a point they proved when disaster struck in the sixth minute.

I almost had the ball in the net after just thirty seconds but it was cleared off the line by a defender. Then, five minutes later, as we hunted for the aggregate equaliser a harmless-looking ball was floated up to Alan Gilzean. When he failed to control it the ball fell to Pearce and he flicked it into the net.[8]

The silence inside Fir Park was deafening.

If it wasn't for our fans I think you could have counted us out at that point. We were sick to our collective stomachs. But after the supporters got over the shock a crescendo of noise engulfed us. They wanted to win this match, probably more than any other game they had ever seen. Their passion galvanised us and back we came.

It often wasn't pretty and you couldn't help but compare their inch-perfect passing with our more wayward distribution but we got the bit between our teeth and, in the thirty-ninth minute, Dixie made good on his pre-match pledge to make Mike England look ordinary yet again. He brilliantly beat the big stopper and sent Brian Heron away and running down the left. Brian left Joe Kinnear for dead and then, from an impossible angle, lashed the ball into the net past keeper Ken Hancock (who was in for the injured Jennings). It was a goal worthy of winning a cup final.

After that, just like at White Hart Lane a fortnight earlier, we got better as the game wore on and I must pay tribute here to the man I always think of as 'Mr Motherwell': Joe Wark, who put in a shift that had to be seen to be believed. I don't think a Spurs player got the better of him the whole night. Many chances were made and many were spurned and we were also denied a blatant penalty when Mike England pulled down Jumbo Muir. Keith MacRae was once again

---

[8]   Some reports give the goal to Chivers.

outstanding and he pulled off yet another wonder save from Alan Gilzean to keep us in the tie. But we floored them with a double whammy: Tom Donnelly hit a screamer from thirty yards to level the tie then Bobby Watson scored with another long-range effort to give us an aggregate lead of 5–4. After that, try as they might, Spurs couldn't find an equaliser and at the end of the ninety minutes we had taken one of the biggest scalps imaginable.

How we celebrated in that dressing room. In fact we were still jumping around when a familiar figure walked into the midst of the chaos. It was Jock Stein, who wanted to be the first to congratulate Bobby Howitt and his team. He was really pleased for us and I thought to myself that it was a wonderful gesture from a real football man.

The press used up every superlative in the book, and then some, to describe our performance. The *Daily Record* was typical and under the headline, 'THE MAGIC WELL' it gushed: 'Motherwell the magnificent, Motherwell the marvellous . . . it was one of the most glorious victories in their long and colourful history.' I have to agree. I thought we were outstanding that night.

There was a bizarre and rather frightening incident after the final whistle. The number of people who had been at the game was so great that when fans were leaving the stadium many had to climb over the players' cars to escape the crush. It wasn't vandalism; they would have been seriously injured, or worse, had they not taken evasive action. The simple fact was that the crowd was too big to be safely accommodated and having seen at close quarters how people were squeezed in I would have put a higher figure on it than the official 22,000. It is certainly the case that an attendance of that magnitude would not be allowed today given the strict health-and-safety standards that are now applied. Poor Davie Whiteford had just bought a new car and it got badly damaged. I had just acquired a second-hand job and when I came out after getting changed I found that the roof had been caved in. Fair play to the club. When we spoke to them about it we all got compensation for the damage that had been done. The important thing of course was that no one was seriously hurt, although it could so easily have been a disaster.

With Stoke and Spurs vanquished we really didn't care who we got in the last four. As luck would have it we drew Hearts, which I suppose at least guaranteed that a Scottish club would be in the final. I didn't think we had anything to fear from the men from Tynecastle; we finished above them in the league that season and after our heroics in earlier rounds surely nothing was beyond us. The first leg, on 16 December 1970, was at Tynecastle and we went through to Edinburgh full of confidence, despite the fact that they had just beaten us at Fir Park in a league fixture on the Saturday.

The game was not unlike our away ties against Stoke and Spurs, with the home team dominant in the first half and us coming more into it in the second half. Despite considerable pressure they went in at half time just one up, a stunning shot from their star striker, Donald Ford, who had scored both their goals in the league game. But once again we gave a much better account of ourselves in the second half. Our equaliser came from Jumbo Muir, who had an excellent game, and the game ended 1–1, setting us up nicely for the second leg, which, strangely, was not until March.

By the time the game came around it was, for us, the only show in town. We had been humbled in the Scottish Cup by lower-league opposition (Stirling Albion beat us 3–1) and had all but settled for the respectability of a mid-table finish in the league. So the semi-final was even more keenly anticipated than normal by players and fans alike. A huge crowd turned up, more than 25,000, and with many of them from Edinburgh, the atmosphere was every bit as good as for the Spurs game.

However, what the fans witnessed, in my opinion, was daylight robbery. There is no other way to describe it.

We performed superbly with every man jack of us putting in a real shift. Our domination was near total in the first period but we just couldn't breach their defensive wall, in which keeper Jim Cruickshank was outstanding. It was the same story at the start of the second half but this time we got our just rewards. After a great pass from Kirkie Lawson the ball was turned into the net by Brian Heron to put us 2–1 ahead on aggregate. After that we were comfortable and all Hearts could offer was a succession of nasty fouls, borne no doubt out of frustration as the tie slipped away.

Deep into injury time, with our fans whistling furiously for time up, we got a goal kick after the ball had been put out of play by Brown, one of their forwards, in what was surely the Gorgie men's last attack. But to the surprise of everyone in the ground, including the Hearts players, Mr Paterson, the referee, inexplicably decided to overrule his linesman and awarded them a corner. When the corner came in we made innumerable attempts to clear but with twenty-one bodies inside a packed penalty area the ball just kept bouncing off people. It was a strange feeling, as if everything was happening in slow motion, despite our increasingly frantic attempts to boot the ball out of the box. I thought we had finally got out of danger when our keeper, Billy Ritchie, made an instinctive save from Ford but as luck would have it the ball fell nicely for their substitute, George Fleming, who drove it home from point-blank range.

The wind taken out of your sails; the stuffing knocked out of you; kicked in the teeth. Choose you own cliché. They all applied to us at that moment. It was a ridiculous decision by Paterson to give Hearts a corner and it cost us a place in the final.

It was now obvious to everyone that Hearts would go on and win the tie and sure enough they did. Donald Ford, their best player over the two legs, got the winner in extra time (a fine goal it was) and we were out. I don't think I have ever felt so sick at any point in my long career in football. As we trooped dejectedly off the pitch the stadium announcer for reasons known only to himself elected to play 'The Carnival is Over' by The Seekers. Talk about rubbing salt into the wound.

I knew that Linda would be upset too, not because we lost but because I had promised to buy her a new fridge-freezer with my win bonus! But that little domestic problem apart the debacle of the corner-that-never-was still haunts me to this day. We sweated blood to get to that semi-final and to have it snatched away by a decision like that is simply unacceptable. I know that anyone who has played the game professionally would feel the same way.

If you think that is sour grapes on my part consider what the papers said. The *Motherwell Times* thought we had been treated abominably by Mr Paterson; you would expect that. But the *Daily Record*, not known as a mouthpiece for Motherwell Football Club, couldn't have been clearer. In the match report it says: 'To me it looked as if Brown had put the ball over himself. But the referee awarded a corner.' After observing that Motherwell had been on top for the regulation ninety minutes the *Record* concludes 'No one will doubt Hearts were the luckiest team in the world to be in the Texaco final.'

And so say all of us.

I ran into Mr Paterson in the mid 1980s in, of all places, a lift at Ibrox. He was there in his capacity as a referee supervisor (Motherwell fans will be wondering how the hell he got that job). Fifteen years had passed since that fateful night at Fir Park but when the doors slid open and he walked in the bad memories came flooding back. I was still angry about what had happened, angrier than I had perhaps realised, and I asked him if he remembered the game. I can't recall what he said but I do remember giving him stick. I tried to make it sound as if I was making a joke of it but underneath I was livid.

* * *

Putting the disappointment of losing to Hearts to one side I suppose it was a great achievement for a club like Motherwell to beat the likes of Stoke and Spurs and reach the semis. It would be unthinkable now for a provincial Scottish side to take on English Premiership opposition and beat them over two legs but the fact of the matter is that we didn't fear those clubs and while we knew they would be favourites to progress we still thought we had a real chance.

Scottish football was very strong at that time. We all know about the successes of the Sixties but there were many glory nights in the early Seventies as well. Both Celtic and Rangers performed heroically, going deep into European competitions on a regular basis. The year after our Texaco run, in 1971/72, Dundee knocked Cologne out of the UEFA Cup before losing narrowly to AC Milan while St Johnstone also had a great run after eliminating German giants Hamburg in the first round. I could list other examples but you get the picture.

The Scottish game has fallen a long way since then: but why? I don't pretend to have the answers but one reason must be the lack of investment in training facilities and in coaching, especially for young players. We should have spent the money in the good times but we were,

I think, just too complacent. While other countries were spending heavily we sat on our hands and let them catch up and then overtake us. I don't know if my experiences at Motherwell were typical but I think they are worth considering.

I have already talked about the rather basic facilities and routines that were used to train part-time players at Motherwell, particularly the emphasis on running and fitness, which were too often a substitute for practising technique and ball work. When I turned full time I thought, perhaps naively, that things would get better. That wasn't the case. The full-time players used to train on a tarmacadam area outside the stadium that is quite close to Motherwell College. The hard surface was hardly ideal for an athlete and it was of course the polar opposite of the grass pitches we were expected to perform on come Saturday afternoons. How you were supposed to hone your skills on tarmac I will never know.

While the terrible facilities were a sad indictment of the whole of Scottish football there were specific circumstances at Fir Park that I felt didn't help. They called into question just how seriously the club took training and preparation.

Step forward 'Jimmy the Mini'.

Jimmy was a Church of Scotland minister (hence his nickname 'Mini') in Motherwell. He was a football fanatic who was not only a regular at Fir Park but also a keen amateur player who turned out in the local churches league. The problem was that after he had seen to his duties in the Kirk he turned up at Fir Park and took part in our training sessions. It was totally unreal. We couldn't even curse in peace because Jimmy brought in a swear box, which no doubt helped to swell the fund for replacing the roof on his church!

Jimmy the Mini came to our place of work on a regular basis but he also tried to get us into his place of work as often as he could! I remember one time he organised a sportsman's service at a church in Hamilton, at which the members of the Hamilton Caley bowling club acted as the choir. My teammate Bobby Watson, himself a committed Christian, was to give the sermon while I was roped into giving a Bible reading. Public speaking is not something that comes naturally to me and when I saw that the church was packed to capacity it made me even more apprehensive.

Bobby must have noticed how nervous I was because as Jimmy was conducting the service he whispered to me:

'How are you feeling?'

'The sweat's running down the shuch of my arse,' I replied, as quietly as possible.

Of course what did Bobby do? He told the congregation what I had said – yes, word for word! I will never know how I managed to give that reading. It was more nerve-racking than playing Spurs.

That of course is a light-hearted little anecdote but the points I make about facilities and coaching are valid. We should have put an infrastructure in place in the good times rather than assuming that the conveyor belt of talent would be never-ending. I don't think that as a nation we have ever taken coaching and practising as seriously as we should, relying instead on our natural passion for the game and our undoubted will to win. That has begun to change but only really in the last ten years and we now have a mountain to climb if we are to catch up with the facilities on offer in other European countries.

6

A Call to Dark ... and Light Blue

While the league will always be a player's bread and butter I have no doubt that my performances in the Texaco Cup and in high-profile domestic cup competitions convinced Scotland manager Bobby Brown that I was capable of doing a job for my country. These are the games that make people sit up and take notice. My first call-up was not to the full international squad but for the under-23s in a game against England at Hampden on 24 February 1971. I was delighted. It had always been a dream of mine to pull on that dark-blue jersey and the fact that we were playing our greatest rivals made it extra special.

As you might expect the England team was very strong with the likes of Ray Clemence, Colin Todd, Tony Currie and Larry Lloyd in its ranks. But young Scotland was also a talented bunch with Sandy Jardine, Davie Hay, George Connelly and Arthur Duncan among the luminaries. I was picked to play on the left side of midfield in a three-man unit that had Eddie Kelly of Arsenal on the right and Davie Robb of Aberdeen in the middle.

Scotland: MacRae, Jardine, Hay, Blackley, Connelly, Kelly, Young, Forsyth, Robb, Jarvie, Duncan

The general consensus was that we played superbly, going in 2–0 up at half-time despite John Blackley (of Hibs) missing a penalty. Although we slackened off in the second half, allowing them to score twice and to snatch an undeserved 2–2 draw, the press was full of praise. The *Evening Times* was typical: 'The young Scots were magnificent . . . Scottish international football renewed a long-lost acquaintanceship with superlatives via our under-23 team,' it gushes. My performance was also given top marks, with the *Times* describing me as the 'find of the night', which was nice to hear if just a little over the top.

It was my first taste of representative honours and I relished every minute of the build-up and the game itself. I felt I had done myself justice – against top opposition – and hoped to feature again for Scotland before long.

I got my wish less than a month later. I was picked for the league international at Hampden, also against England. With so many fine footballers available to Bobby Brown, including a fair sprinkling of Old Firm players, I wasn't sure if I would get in the side. Fortunately for me I chose the Saturday before the big game at Hampden to score the best goal of my career. Motherwell were playing Falkirk in the league and during the game I embarked on a mazy run that left several defenders in my wake before sending an unstoppable shot past the Bairns keeper from thirty yards. Described by one paper as a 'flash of genius' it was the stuff dreams are made of and because the television cameras were present the whole nation saw it, including the one viewer who mattered more than any other: Mr Bobby Brown esquire! How could he leave me out after that?

Sure enough I was in the starting eleven – again in a midfield role – which was an even bigger thrill than the under-23 match. They had some class players: Bobby Moore, Geoff Hurst, Roy McFarland, Paul Reaney, John Hollins; this was no reserve team. Scotland on the other hand had been badly hit by call-offs, with several Old Firm stalwarts declaring themselves unfit.

Scotland: Clark, Jardine, Hay, Forsyth, McKinnon, Brogan, McLean, Callaghan, Robb, Jarvie, Ford

We played reasonably well but just couldn't put our chances away and England won 1–0 thanks to an early strike from Ralph Coates. Despite my two performances in dark blue meeting with general approval I was disappointed not to be selected for Scotland's European Championship qualifier against Portugal in April 1971.[9] My debut as

---

9   Maybe it was just as well I was not called upon because Scotland went down to a 2–0 defeat, virtually ending our hopes of qualification for the finals.

a full international, however, was just weeks away. Thanks to the withdrawal of a whole raft of players for what was essentially a meaningless game I was called up for the next qualifier, which was against Denmark in Copenhagen on 9 June 1971. While I was honoured to be chosen the problem was that, not expecting to be called upon, I hadn't played or trained for about seven weeks. As soon as I was given the news I began to train, on my own, but that is no substitute for supervised sessions and competitive matches.

Scotland: Clark, Munro, Dickson, Stanton, McKinnon, Moncur, McLean, Forsyth, Stein, Curran, Forrest

Despite my best efforts my lack of sharpness was a real problem and the game with the Danes turned out to be one of the most disappointing nights of my life. You have to bear in mind that Denmark were not the force that they would become. In 1992 of course they won the European Championships and in the recent past they have qualified for the World Cup on several occasions. But they were an amateur side until the early 1970s – with professionals banned from playing for the national team – and were more used to playing in the Olympic Games. Perhaps understandably, the Scottish media did not rate them, with one newspaper disparagingly describing them as the 'country cousins of international football'. They hadn't won a game for three years and even that was against Finland, another team considered one of the whipping boys of European football.

But that night our 'country cousins', playing with great determination and spirit, were just too good for us. They won 1–0 thanks to a stunning free kick struck from twenty yards by Finn Laudrup, the father of Michael and Brian, both of whom would perform at the highest level in club and international football. I had been paired with Pat Stanton in the midfield and I have to confess that I had a stinker. After all the praise I had been getting for my performances for club and country I was brought back down to earth with a bang, with one journalist describing me as 'out of touch'. I knew the reason for my poor performance was lack of fitness but that is invariably overlooked when you have a bad game. Whatever the reason for my poor showing I felt really low on the flight back to Scotland, believing that I had let myself and my country down.

Thanks to that game and injuries sustained in domestic football it would be two-and-a-bit years before I played for Scotland again and five years before I could count on a regular place in the side. I was called up for squads, and was on the bench for the 1973 clash with England at Wembley, but I never got on the pitch apart from one game against Czechoslovakia in 1974. Along the way I missed most of the qualifying campaign for the 1974 World Cup and the finals. It just shows the effect that one bad game can have on your career.

* * *

Despite the disappointment of that night in Copenhagen I look back on seasons 1970/71 and 1971/72 as two of my best. I had cemented myself in the Motherwell team (as a centre back); I had played a prominent part in the Texaco Cup run; I had represented Scotland at three levels in the same season.

Then when I thought life couldn't get any better it did. On 12 October 1972 I signed for Rangers.

There had been speculation about my future for what seemed like an age. It was a case of another week, another rumour. I knew that Dundee, Blackpool and Nottingham Forest were interested, as was Bill Shankly of Liverpool, and stories to that effect appeared with great regularity in the papers. There was talk too of Celtic, who had shown some interest when I was with the Violet.

It is flattering when other clubs are looking at you but when Rangers made their interest known I was elated. I was delighted to have played for Stonehouse and then to have moved to the seniors with Motherwell. But signing for a club of that stature was a huge thrill. As a boy I had dreamt of playing for a top side and of course I had always had a soft spot for Rangers. Although the period from Rangers showing their hand until I signed was probably only a matter of weeks it seemed like an age, which speaks volumes about my desire to go to Ibrox. It wasn't made any easier by the gentlemen of the press. One journalist in particular phoned me on what seemed like a daily basis to find out if the transfer was imminent. Every time the phone rang I thought it was Motherwell to say that a fee had been agreed and to get myself along to Ibrox.

Then the call came. Motherwell had accepted a bid of £40,000 and I was free to talk to Rangers. After all the speculation I was finally to become a light blue. No one had agents in those days so I went to Ibrox with my father-in-law, Tom Barr. I was, quite naturally, very excited but there was business to be transacted and contract terms to be agreed. It would have been so easy to have been seduced by the grandeur and glamour of Ibrox, not to mention overawed by meeting men like Willie Waddell and Jock Wallace, and to have signed up to the first offer that Rangers made. But Tom was too canny for that. He turned down their first proposal and pushed hard for the best deal he could get. After some quite intense negotiations the deal was sealed. My basic was £90 per week with a lump-sum of £1,000 as a signing-on fee. In 2010 that wage would be a relative pittance but forty years ago it was a lot of money, especially when fairly generous win bonuses – much more likely at Rangers than at Motherwell – were added to the mix.

To be honest, at that precise moment in time the money was a secondary consideration. I had just fulfilled the ambition of a lifetime. That was what really mattered.

At the same time I was grateful for all that Motherwell had done for me and I would certainly miss Fir Park and the supporters. I think most of them understood why I was leaving and let's face it Motherwell made a huge profit on me, no small consideration for a provincial club. Some fans however were upset, really angry, feeling that somehow I had left them in the lurch. I expected to get stick any time I went back there with Rangers and that is exactly what happened. However, I didn't anticipate that people would still be raising the issue decades later. Only last year, in 2009, I was at a lunch in the Vice-President's club at Fir Park with my old Motherwell teammates. I was chatting amiably to some of the other guests when one of them, a member of the VP club, made a quite remarkable comment to me.

'You and Gregor Stevens became monsters when you signed for Rangers,' he said.

I couldn't believe that after all the years that had passed he would say a thing like that. I just laughed, went over to my table and sat down for lunch.

7

The Centenary Cup Final and *that* Goal

After all the feverish speculation, the sleepless nights and the hours spent waiting for a phone call telling me I was Ibrox bound my big day had finally arrived. *I was a Ranger.* I can't begin to describe how good those words sounded. I had waited my whole life for this moment. I knew that thousands, probably millions, of people of a light-blue persuasion would have given their right arms to swap places with me. Now it was up to me to prove that I was good enough to fill that famous jersey.

I am afraid that things didn't start well. My debut, on 14 October 1972, was against, of all teams, Motherwell at Fir Park and it wasn't the most auspicious. I found it hard to play against my old teammates. It was a strange feeling. The previous week I had been alongside them in claret and amber. Now I was up against them. However, my rather tentative performance didn't seem to affect my new colleagues and we left Lanarkshire with a 2–0 win thanks to goals from Cutty Young and Derek Parlane.

I was selected again for the next two league games but then I pulled a muscle at training and was out for two months. That was a real sickener. I had been virtually injury free during my time at Motherwell and now after getting my dream move I was to be consigned to the sidelines. I knew only too well that with the players at Jock Wallace's disposal I might not come straight back in after being given the all-clear by the medical staff. I was also missing a big chunk of games in what promised to be one of the tightest league-title races for years, with the two Old Firm clubs well clear of the pack and going at it hammer and tong right from the off. I shouldn't have worried. That season turned out to be one of the most momentous of my career. I not only re-established myself in the Rangers team but also played against the greatest player in the world – twice.

Oh, and for good measure, I just happened to score the most famous goal in the history of the Scottish Cup.

I came back for a league game on 23 December 1972, in the side that beat East Fife 4–0. It was the start of a remarkable run in the championship, one in which we went unbeaten for eighteen games, winning seventeen and drawing one. In any other season, in any other country, that would have been title-winning form but we were pipped at the post by Celtic, who were able to field one of the strongest sides in their history. We really did take it to the proverbial wire and for much of the early part of 1973 we were two points in front at the top of the league, although Celtic always had a game in hand. Our downfall came at Pittodrie on 21 April. Watched by an amazing crowd of 33,000 it was a hard-fought game in which Peter McCloy produced one of his best-ever performances in a Rangers jersey. He pulled off a string of incredible saves and we left the north-east with a highly creditable two-two draw.

Sadly, it would not be enough. Celtic, having already won their game in hand, took two points that afternoon, propelling them to the top of the table. If they beat Hibs at Easter Road the following Saturday in the final round of matches they would be champions once again. That's how it turned out. We did our part by beating East Fife at home but the men from the east of the city beat Hibs comfortably to finish on fifty-seven points to our fifty-six.

It really was that close.

* * *

Away from the domestic game there was an intriguing clash with Ajax. They were the European Cup holders and as Rangers had won the

European Cup Winners Cup in 1972 it was agreed by the two clubs that they would meet on a home-and-away basis for an unofficial European Super Cup. At the time it was considered a novel idea but the super-cup concept has, of course, since been taken up by UEFA. It would be our only involvement in European competition in 1972/73. The club had been served with a year's ban by UEFA thanks to the pitch invasion in Barcelona after the Cup Winners Cup final.

I was thrilled about the prospect of facing Ajax. They had elevated themselves into the pantheon of European football by winning the European Cup for the second year running in 1972 with a comprehensive defeat of Inter Milan.[10] It wasn't just the fact of their winning that excited me; it was the way they won. Ajax played a wonderful brand of fast, attacking football that appealed to the football purist. Who wouldn't want to watch, or play against, guys like Neeskens, Haan, Muhren and Krol? And let's not forget the most eminent Dutch master of them all, Johann Cruyff, one of the greatest players in history and then at the peak of his powers. It was no surprise to anyone when they won the European Cup for the third time in a row later in 1973, knocking out CSKA Sofia, Bayern Munich and Real Madrid along the way before defeating Juventus in the final. If there was a better team on the planet it would have been news to me.

The first leg was at Ibrox, in January 1973, and sixty thousand Rangers fans turned out to watch us take on the mighty Dutchmen. We lost by three goals to one, but that was no disgrace against a team of that calibre. Cruyff, as I expected, was magnificent and he put on a real master class. I have never faced anyone who was so quick over short distances. If the Olympic sprint was decided by a five-metre race this guy would have won the gold medal hands down. His touch and awareness were also exceptional and I will never forget the goal he scored that night. He received the ball about twenty-five yards from our goal and as I tried to get a tackle in he beat me on my left and then for good measure he beat me on my right as well. A split second later

---

[10] Ajax would add the 1972 World Club Championship to their impressive haul of honours.

he had imperiously volleyed the ball into our net past a helpless Peter McCloy. I was never happy about conceding a goal, especially after I had been turned inside out by the scorer, but I have to say it was one of the finest sequences I have ever witnessed on a football field.

We probably played better in the return leg in Amsterdam, scoring twice through Cutty Young and Alex MacDonald to make it 2–2 at half time. But Cruyff was once again the main difference between the teams, scoring the winner in the second half.

The man was a genius, the best player I ever faced.

* * *

The Scottish Cup, inaugurated by the Scottish Football Association in 1873, is the oldest national cup competition in the world. With the 1972/73 final being designated as the centenary final there was even more incentive than usual for Rangers to win it. It also looked entirely possible that it might be our only chance of lifting silverware. We had been knocked out of the League Cup at the semi-final stage (a competition for which I was cup-tied having already played in an earlier round for Motherwell), there was the ever-present possibility of Celtic pipping us at the post for the league title and of course we had been denied the opportunity of playing in Europe's official competitions.

Lady Luck certainly did not smile on us in terms of the draws we were handed. Every team we faced that year was in the first division: two of them would finish in the top three while two of the others would finish in the upper half of the league. First up was Dundee United at Ibrox. United knocked the ball about beautifully on the day, frustrating us by keeping possession and, when we had the ball, by defending in numbers. Their star men that day were the future Rangers management duo of Walter Smith and Archie Knox, both of whom played superbly. But in the second half we began to wear them down and laid siege to their goal. The breakthrough came after sixty-four minutes when Cutty Young scored the only goal of the game.

If anything the draw for the fourth round was even tougher. We were followed out of the hat by Hibs, the best team in the country outside of the Old Firm. The game was played in February but I will always remember running out onto the park in perfect sunshine to be greeted by a huge crowd of 63,889. In the first half we were dominant but despite creating several good chances we went in at half time leading just 1–0, courtesy of a Derek Johnstone strike. Inevitably, those missed chances came back to haunt us as Hibs, inspired by their captain, Pat Stanton, roared back in the second half. As I record elsewhere in this book (in the course of an anecdote about Jock Wallace) I managed to lose their powerful centre forward, Alan Gordon, at a corner and he took full advantage to nod home the equaliser.[11]

The midweek replay at Easter Road also attracted an amazing attendance – 49,007, no less – and they were treated to a cup tie that had everything: great goals, wonderful football and controversy by the bucket-load. In the eyes of many pundits Hibs – led by the inspirational Stanton, who was in the form of his life – were the favourites to progress. That wasn't how we saw it and in six minutes we were ahead thanks to a wonderful goal from Tommy McLean. He accepted a great pass from Derek Parlane, controlled the ball instantly, rounded keeper Jim Herriot and calmly put us one-nil up. Hibs and their supporters were stunned but gradually they edged their way back into the game and with Stanton directing operations they pushed us further and further back. I don't think many teams could have kept them at bay but we managed it for an hour with a resolute, backs-to-the-wall defensive performance that included a string of world-class saves from Peter McCloy. Despite the heroics we couldn't hold them forever and after sixty-five minutes Arthur Duncan equalised with the second great goal of the night.

Given the impetus that a goal in front of your own supporters normally brings, most observers would have expected Hibs to go on and win the tie but we continued to look dangerous on the break and when Derek Parlane was upended after bursting into the box every Rangers fan inside Easter Road shouted 'penalty'. Referee Bobby Davidson seemed unsure about what to do so he ran over to consult his linesman. With close to fifty thousand people holding their breath

---

[11] See page 92.

he and his colleague discussed the pros and cons of the claim for what seemed an eternity. Then he turned, ran back to the box and pointed to the penalty spot.

The Hibs players, who clearly thought Derek had dived, were outraged by the decision and harried Davidson for all they were worth. But he would not budge, and, amidst the tumult of angry protests from Hibs, Tommy McLean lined up to take the spot kick. He was as cool as you like and comfortably swept the ball home to give us the lead. There was yet more controversy in the dying minutes when Hibs vehemently protested to Mr Davidson that I had pushed Alan Gordon off the ball inside the box but despite the obvious temptation to cancel out his earlier contentious decision by awarding the second penalty of the night he waved play on. We were then able to play time out to secure what was probably our hardest-fought victory of the entire season.

The quarter-final was more straightforward. We played Airdrie at Ibrox, and with Tommy McLean again outstanding, beat them comfortably by two goals to nil. With Celtic also in the semi-final it seemed to be written in the stars that we would be kept apart in the draw, leaving open the mouth-watering prospect of an Old Firm centenary final. That's how it panned out. We were paired with Ayr United and we did of course reach the final but not before being given a hell of a fright by the Honest Men.

This was not the Ayr United of today, a club struggling to keep its head above water in the darker recesses of the Scottish Football League. This was a vibrant, combative, in-your-face, top-half-of-the-first-division outfit. Ayr had already beaten us in the league that year and in the quarter finals they had hammered Partick Thistle 5–1. They were led by one of the most confident managers ever to pull on a sheepskin jacket. From his vantage point in the dugout Ally MacLeod would expend almost as much energy as his players. He was a dervish; jumping up and down, cajoling his players, berating the referee, kicking every ball. It was also the first time Ayr had been in the Scottish Cup semi-final and I was sure that having got this far they would not give in without a hell of a fight. Ally would see to that.

On a wet April night Ayr came flying out of the traps and before a minute had elapsed we were in trouble. Their young full back Davy Wells floated in a free kick, which was met by Ayr's tough-as-teak centre forward Alex 'Dixie' Ingram (a man I had many jousts with). Dixie, as his nickname suggests, was excellent in the air and he fairly bulleted a header past Peter McCloy. One-nil down in the semi-final of the Scottish Cup and with some of our fans yet to pass through the Hampden turnstiles; this was most definitely not in the script.

Then all hell broke loose.

The linesman raised his flag, indicating that Ingram was offside, and referee Bobby Davidson chalked off the goal. The Ayr players, especially Ingram, were raging, while Ally MacLeod as you might expect was apoplectic, but despite their protests Davidson would not budge. His decision would reignite the perennial debate about the Old Firm being favoured by referees. I had seen it from both sides of the fence. At Motherwell I was in no doubt: Celtic and Rangers invariably got the lion's share of the decisions when an official was faced with a close call. But when I moved to Ibrox I began to have doubts. Through-out the course of a season Rangers would be on the receiving end of many bad calls but people would tend to discount them, perhaps because they thought it was poetic justice for all the ones that allegedly went in our favour.

Whatever the answer is to that age-old conundrum we went on to win the game 2–0, thanks to a brace from Derek Parlane. I could now look forward to a game that would by some distance be the biggest of my career.

After the league campaign had ended the club took us away for a few days to Turnberry hotel, a luxury establishment on the Ayrshire coast with a range of fine golf courses and of course a venue for the Open championship. With an Old Firm Scottish Cup final the following Saturday Jock felt that a few days away from the goldfish bowl of Ibrox would do us the world of good and also help with team bonding. It turned out to be one hell of a trip.

On the first night, a Saturday, we were having a drink in the Turnberry bar. Big Jock was on the bell.

'What do you want to drink son?' he asked.

As a new boy at Rangers I thought I would try to impress him with my moderation when it came to alcohol.

'I'll have a half pint of lager boss,' I replied

Jock was having none of it.

'Just have a pint like a man, son,' he growled.

One night we went to a pub in in Maidens, the nearest village to Turnberry. I don't know if it was a case of letting off steam after a hard season or drowning our sorrows after losing the title by such a narrow margin, but, whatever the reason we really tied one on. The drink flowed and it didn't stop flowing for the rest of the night. We had a great time, so much so that when I looked at my watch I was shocked to discover it was already one o'clock in the morning. No wonder the publican looked so worried. He probably thought he would never get us out.

Poor Joe Mason was the fall guy. The boys whipped off his trousers and hid them somewhere he would never find them. The result was that Joe had to go back to our ever-so-posh, five-star hotel and ask for his room key with just a pair of Y-fronts to cover his modesty! He was lucky it was so late because it meant there were no other guests around. By this point there were only about five of us left in the hotel lobby. We must have been making a bit of a racket because we woke up one of the guests.

The problem for us was that the guest in question was Jock Wallace.

He strode down the stairs and into the lobby.

'Get to your beds. I'll see you all in the morning.'

And see us in the morning he did. We got a bollocking and a fine for our troubles.

I didn't mind that much. It had been a great trip. Although everyone had made me very welcome since my transfer from Motherwell this was my first extended trip away with the boys and I feel it helped me to get to know them better. If that had been Jock's intention it worked.

We were ready for Celtic.

* * *

The 1973 Scottish Cup final, played on 5 May, is special for many reasons. It was a double centenary. The SFA was founded in 1873 and the game was therefore designated as the centenary final for that reason.[12] It was also the centenary of Rangers Football Club, as the club had been officially founded in 1873.[13] It was the first royal final, with Princess Alexandra, the Queen's cousin, in attendance. Showbiz royalty – led by Sean Connery who was then still a Celtic fan according to the press – also put in an appearance. Then there was the attendance: at 122,714 it is a record of a kind, as it was the last time that a crowd in excess of 100,000 gathered to watch a game in Scotland.

But there is another reason that the game was special. The number of quality players who took part.

Rangers: McCloy, Jardine, Mathieson, Greig, Johnstone, Mac-Donald, McLean, Forsyth, Parlane, Conn, Young

Celtic: Hunter, McGrain, Brogan, Murdoch, McNeill, Connelly, Johnstone, Deans, Dalglish, Hay, Callaghan

It is very hard to spot a weakness in either team. The only guys I didn't pick for my Rangers dream team[14] from our eleven that afternoon are Parlane, Conn and Young, but they were three highly talented individuals who made a great contribution in their time at Ibrox. Derek Parlane was our top goal-scorer four times, Alfie Conn was a skilful midfielder and Quinton 'Cutty' Young was a fast, direct winger who had always given us trouble when he played for Ayr United.

The Celtic team that day can lay claim, I believe, to being one of the strongest in their history. It had three Lisbon Lions (Murdoch, McNeill and Johnstone), four of Celtic's so-called Quality Street Kids (McGrain, Dalglish, Hay and Connelly) and four other excellent players in Ally Hunter, Jim Brogan, Dixie Deans and Tommy Callaghan. Goalkeeper Hunter was a Scotland international; Brogan had played in the 1970 European Cup final; Deans's talents I knew well from my days alongside him at Fir Park; while Tommy Callaghan was so highly rated by Jock Stein that he signed him twice.

---

12 It wasn't of course the centenary of the Scottish Cup final, as some people mistakenly refer to it. The first Scottish Cup competition took place in season 1873/74 and the final, won by Queen's Park, was played in 1874.

13 Some Rangers fans prefer 1872 as the inaugural year as that was when Moses McNeil and the other founders played their first game.

14 See pages 173–8.

We were introduced to the Princess on the pitch before the game, which gave the Rangers fans the opportunity to launch into a heartfelt rendition of 'God Save the Queen'. Then with the pleasantries done it was time for the action.

It was a pulsating game, full of end-to-end football, swinging one way then the other. Celtic scored first through Dalglish before Derek Parlane equalised in the thirty-fifth minute to send the teams in for the half-time break level at 1–1. The second half followed the same pattern with both teams committing men forward at every opportunity. We went ahead through Alfie Conn before George Connelly levelled things again from the penalty spot.

Then after sixty-one minutes we got a free kick. The ball was expertly lofted into the box by Tommy McLean and found the head of Derek Johnstone, who guided a header goal-ward. The ball hit the post, dropped to the ground, rolled along the goal line and hit the other post. I was in the box just a few feet away and my immediate reaction was that the ball was going in. I was so sure that I stood there trans-fixed for what seemed like an age, but in reality was only a split second. Then a thought flashed through my mind.

'I have to make sure.'

Having lost my marker, Dixie Deans, I stuck my leg out and managed to prod the ball over the line. It was my first-ever goal for Rangers. What happened next is a blur. I am told I went on a mazy run to celeb-rate my goal but I have no recollection of it. I was in ecstasy, as were the sixty-odd thousand bluenoses in the crowd. Up in the old centre stand Linda, pregnant with our first child, was looking on. She leapt up with such abandon that Beth McLean, the wife of Tommy, was worried about the welfare of our unborn baby. Fortunately, mother and child suffered no ill effects from the celebrations!

My goal, putting us 3–2 in front, was enough to win the Cup. It was a wonderful day for the club, enjoyed by fans and players alike, and boy how the whole Rangers family celebrated that night. John Lawrence, one paper reported, was in tears after the game, telling reporters that 'it was the greatest night in the history of the club'. That might have been a slight exaggeration but it shows you how much it meant to everyone of a light-blue persuasion to win an Old Firm cup final, especially when we had won only one domestic trophy in the past seven years.

There are so many myths and misperceptions about my goal. To this day people come up to me and say: 'You nearly missed it.' But that is because the newspaper reports got it wrong, with some headlines the next day claiming that Tom Forsyth nearly missed it. How the journalists came to that conclusion is a mystery to me. They must have been confused by the length of time it took me to knock the ball in, which of course is a completely different issue.

We deserved to win the Scottish Cup that afternoon. The team matched Celtic in every area of the field and, in some, surpassed them. Although they were still the dominant side in Scotland we had laid down a marker. We had shown we were up for the challenge in both league and cup. We would not overtake them immediately yet slowly but surely we were gaining ground.

Rangers were back.

8

The Nightmare Is Over:
Stopping Ten-in-a-Row

Neither half of the Old Firm can accept the team on the other side of the city sweeping all before it for any length of time. The pressure from supporters and the media simply becomes irresistible, forcing the club suffering the losing streak to change, often in ways it finds unpalatable. New players will be brought in, managers and coaches sacked and in some cases even the ownership of the club will pass into new hands. So it was with Rangers in the summer of 1974. Celtic had won – I hate to say it – nine championships in a row and for good measure had thrown in a European Cup and a few other domestic competitions. Now Jock Stein and his players were overwhelming favourites to make it into double figures, the dreaded ten-in-a-row, a truly horrible prospect for Rangers supporters everywhere.

The club had tried everything. Money had been spent on expensive new recruits, including Colin Stein for whom £100,000 had been paid to Hibs in 1968, shattering the transfer record for a deal involving Scottish clubs. Good managers had been jettisoned as the Celtic juggernaut gathered momentum. Scot Symon – a distinguished former player and a man who had guided the club to fifteen major trophies, including a treble – was cruelly sacked in November 1967 while the team was sitting proudly at the top of the league. His successor, Davie White, a promising young manager, was given less than two seasons in the

Ibrox hot seat before being shown the door. But despite the best efforts of everyone of a blue-and-white persuasion, title after title was won by the men from the east end of Glasgow. We had occasionally done well in cup competitions, including of course in Europe, but to come second or even third best in the championship was simply unacceptable for a club like Rangers. It was hard for me to take so God knows what it must have been like for guys like Greig and Jardine who had been at Ibrox for a much longer period of time.

The season when Celtic won their ninth championship was particularly depressing. We had run them close on several occasions but in 1973/74 we seemed to go backwards. Celtic won the league with quite a bit to spare and we couldn't even finish second as Hibs pipped us for the runners-up spot.[15] Our record in Old Firm games was dismal. We played Celtic five times (twice in the league and three times in the League Cup) losing four and winning just once. The traditional New Year derby at Celtic Park, in January 1974, virtually ended our title hopes as we slipped to a 1–0 defeat, giving Celtic a nine-point lead.

Then, just when I thought things couldn't get any worse, I picked up another injury. It happened in training. I developed severe stomach pains and was rushed to hospital. The club told the press I needed a minor operation and that I would be back within weeks. But it would be seven long months before I would pull on a light-blue jersey again.

It was no great surprise that when the new league campaign kicked off on 31 August 1974 Celtic were once again overwhelming favourites to lift their tenth title on the trot. It seemed that neither the bookies nor the wise men of the press could see past the men in green and white. But Jock Wallace had other ideas. Now firmly ensconced in the manager's chair he had free rein to impose his own methods on the team. During pre-season we had visited Gullane where Jock, with the precision that was second nature after his years in the army, made us run up and down those sand dunes until our lungs were fit to burst. I was now back in full training and wasn't spared the torture. It was

---

[15] Celtic in fact accumulated five more points than us, a fairly hefty margin considering it was only two points for a win in those days.

extremely gruelling but the truth is that it did us the world of good despite what the purists thought.

Although Big Jock didn't make wholesale changes in personnel the watchwords now were commitment and discipline. He wanted guys who would fight their corner, guys who would go through the pain barrier and beyond. It was no surprise that players considered skilful, but perhaps less reliable on the pitch, such as Willie Johnston and Alfie Conn, were allowed to leave. And there is no doubt that his incredible enthusiasm, allied to excellent man-management, rubbed off on us. We wanted to please him and we went the extra mile.

Things just seemed to fall into place. After a rather disappointing draw at Somerset Park against Ally MacLeod's Ayr United in our opening fixture we went on an unbeaten run of eleven games that included some stunning wins, including 6–0 and 6–1 demolitions of Kilmarnock and Dunfermline respectively. Perhaps more importantly we went to Parkhead in September and beat Celtic by the odd goal in three in front of a crowd of 65,000. It was a highly controversial encounter, both on and off the pitch. Two players were ordered off – Jim Brogan of Celtic and Derek Parlane of Rangers – and there were four bookings. On the terracing the atmosphere was, to say the least, volatile. Throughout the game bottles and cans were thrown by rival fans and the fighting at one point even spilled onto the pitch. The police said they made so many arrests that they lost count of the numbers. We were just relieved to get out with the two points.

In the first half of the league campaign we only blotted our copybook twice. At home to Hibs, who were again challenging for the title, in November 1974 we lost 1–0 when a win would have put us five points clear of the Easter Road side and severely dented their championship ambitions. It was no disgrace losing to the men from Easter Road; they were outstanding in the early-to-mid Seventies with guys like Pat Stanton, John Blackley, Arthur Duncan, John Brownlie and Joe Harper, to name but a few, in their side, as well as an outstanding manager in Eddie Turnbull. The other loss came as more of a surprise to some people; we went down 4–3 to Airdrie at Broomfield. It wasn't that much of a surprise to me. I knew from bitter experience during my Motherwell days just how hard it was at that funny little ground. Those lapses cost us dear and as the second Old Firm league encounter drew ever nearer Celtic powered to the top of the league. It meant that we were two points behind them going into the traditional Ne'erday derby on 4 January 1975.

Every Old Firm game is vital, but some are more vital than others. This one was in the latter category. In fact I don't believe it is an exaggeration to say that it was one of the most important of all time. Consider what was at stake for us. If Celtic had won they would have been four points clear with a superior goal difference. More than half the campaign had gone and while it would not have been impossible for us to claw back their lead they would have been long odds-on to become champions. That would have been ten-in-a-row and what a psychological fillip that would have given them. Who knows how many more flags they would have taken after that?

The tension in the run up to the game was palpable. I felt it, the fans felt it; the media hyped it up to unbelievable proportions. Nor did the importance of the game go unnoticed in official circles, especially after the widespread outbreaks of hooliganism that had scarred the corresponding fixture at Celtic Park the previous September. The Chief Constable of Strathclyde Police, David McNee, made an appeal for calm and advised that children should not attend the match unless they were accompanied by an adult. The clubs too had made plans: it was agreed that assistant managers Willie Thornton and Sean Fallon would lead the teams onto the field before kick-off and that at half-time legends George Young and Willie Woodburn (for Rangers) and brothers John and Billy McPhail (for Celtic) were to be introduced to the crowd and would kick autographed balls into the packed terracing. We hoped it would be enough.

As I walked onto the field that day it suddenly occurred to me that this was the biggest game I had ever played in, bigger even than the Scottish Cup final of 1973. There was just so much at stake for both sides. Not that it was easy to think clearly. Despite the pouring rain the noise created by the 71,000 shoehorned into Ibrox was deafening; they were well up for it and woe-betide any player who wasn't on top of his game. People talk about the Liverpool and Manchester derbies, or their equivalents in Milan and Madrid, but for noise and spectacle I don't think there is a club game in the world to match the Old Firm.

I looked across at the guys I would be facing. It was a side studded with world-class players: Kenny Dalglish, Danny McGrain, Billy McNeill, Davie Hay. That didn't worry me in the slightest; in fact I found it inspirational. Who could fail to be inspired by playing against guys like that on such an occasion? Especially as we had players that were every bit as good: John Greig, Derek Johnstone, Sandy Jardine, Alex MacDonald, Colin Jackson. (Compare that lot to the boys on show in an Old Firm game today. Yes, I know. Sad, isn't it?)

But it was someone whom I haven't yet mentioned who stole the show that day. A skilful, diminutive, right winger full of tricks . . . and I am not talking here about Jimmy Johnstone. Step forward Tommy McLean, whose finest day it was in a light-blue jersey. Quite simply, the wee man was magnificent. He tore Celtic apart, scoring once and laying on two more for Derek Johnstone and Derek Parlane with pin-point crosses. It was said by one paper that the closest his marker, Jim Brogan, got to Tommy was 'to shake hands after the game'. I was delighted for him, not least because he had come in for some unfair criticism from the boo boys at Ibrox after his transfer from Kilmarnock. As Lanarkshire men we often shared a car together on the daily commute into training and I knew he had been hurt by the criticism.

We ran out winners that day by three goals to nil, a result that put us on top of the league, albeit on goal difference. It was not that Celtic had played badly; in fact they knocked the ball about with a great deal of fluency and but for a few missed chances might well have run us close. But we had a new strength of purpose, a never-say-die attitude that all the great Rangers sides have had. On the day we were just too good for our opponents. The Rangers fans were ecstatic, and despite the pouring rain they refused to leave the stadium until they had belted out every song in the repertoire. In their eyes this was a turning point. We had been under pressure to get a result and we had delivered. Now the sky was the limit.

Of course we still had a lot of work to do but after that win we never faltered and we would not lose again until the last day of the season, long after we had tied up the championship. Although Celtic managed briefly to get back on level terms at the top of the league a sequence of five wins on the trot in February and March, combined with our Old Firm rivals losing three games on the spin, meant that we travelled to Easter Road on 29 March 1975 needing just a point to clinch our first title for eleven years.

We knew it would be tough. The last thing Hibs wanted was for us to clinch the championship in their own backyard. Big Jock told the press and anyone who would listen that 'Easter Road would be no place for fairies'. And how right he was. It was one of the most physical games I have ever played in, punctuated by no less forty fouls and three bookings. I was one of those who had his name taken, being penalised in the thirty-fourth minute after a goalmouth stramash in which Hibs forward Ally McLeod had gone in hard (too hard I felt) on our keeper, Stewart Kennedy.

Hibs actually scored first that day and when Sandy Jardine smacked a penalty off the post I thought we would have to put the champagne on ice for another week. But salvation was at hand. Five minutes later Colin Stein – who had re-signed from Coventry for a fee of £80,000 just three weeks previously – popped up with a header that gave us a 1–1 draw and the title.

Let's get the party started.

Our celebrations, as the *Evening Times* notes, were 'wild, unconfined and genuine'. Our dressing room was stacked high with crates of champagne and let me tell you we didn't waste a drop. We deserved it. We had played out of our skins all season, driven on by the best manager in the business. On the terracing our fans – who made up the majority of the crowd of 38,585 – were in dreamland. Some of them probably thought we would never win the league again in their lifetime. Their long nightmare was over. By way of celebration, they made up a little ditty, which they sang to the tune of hit single 'Magic' by the Scottish band, Pilot.

Oh oh oh
It's magic, you know
Never be ten in a row.

The club meant everything to them. And to me.

It still does.

9

Give a Dog a Bad Name

I decided to call this book Jaws, quite simply because that is how I am often referred to by fans and the media. The Jaws moniker was coined by Allan Herron, the top football writer at the *Sunday Mail* when I was at my peak with Rangers. Herron claims that the idea came to him when forwards hid from me during a game at Ibrox. He was of course making a reference to *Jaws*, the hit film of the 1970s directed by Steven Spielberg, which featured a great white shark that ate unsuspecting bathers at an American seaside resort.

My other nickname, only slightly less over the top, was Iron Man, which had been used to describe me even in my Motherwell days. There was a series on Scottish football's so-called hard men that ran in the *Sunday Mail* in August 1976. It was called 'The Iron Men' and featured a number of players at Scottish clubs, all known, according to the paper, for their reluctance to take prisoners. Pride of place was reserved in the final week of the series for yours truly, the hard man's hard man, or, as the *Mail* describes me, 'the undisputed king of Scotland's hard-hitting defenders'. In an interview for the series Jock Wallace told the *Mail* he had made me his first signing at Ibrox 'because of his strength and aggression. At that time Rangers had too many silky players. We needed someone with his competitive attitude.' When your manager describes you in those terms it is of course grist to the mill of journalists, who seem to go out of their way to pigeonhole footballers, whether as a hard man, or silky smooth or big target man.

Given my press it is little wonder that I got pelters from opposition fans over the years, especially those of the green-and-white variety. Jokes were told to illustrate my predatory instincts:

> The club phoned Tom Forsyth's wife to tell her he was coming home from Europe with a broken leg.
> 'Whose leg is it?' she asked.

Another journalist (John Fairgrieve, also of the *Sunday Mail*) noted, albeit light-heartedly, that such was my reputation that some people saw me as 'not so much a footballer as a reject from Hammer Films – and moreover a reject only because he frightened the life out of Christopher Lee'.

The cartoonists also had fun at my expense. For example, there is one Rod cartoon in the *Daily Record* that shows a player who is about to play against me shaking with fear. By way of explanation the cartoon has the manager turning to his assistant and saying: 'It was a bad time to tell him he was playing against Tom Forsyth. He has just been to see *Jaws*.'

In the court of public opinion I had been tried, found guilty by unanimous verdict and sentenced to life for offences against football. The evidence against me was unambiguous. My sole purpose was to intimidate opposition forwards with crunching tackles, to win the ball before releasing it to a more skilful colleague. I was the Scottish equivalent of Norman 'Bites Your Legs' Hunter or Ron 'Chopper' Harris, who played respectively for Leeds United and Chelsea in the Seventies. I can still reel off the criticism. 'Forsyth was a dirty player, a destroyer,' they cried. 'You only have to look at the number of times he was sent off. It must have been well into double figures. He was never away from Park Gardens.'[16]

They couldn't be more wrong. In a professional career that

---

[16] Park Gardens, in the west end of Glasgow, was the headquarters of the Scottish Football Association when I was a player.

spanned sixteen years I was sent-off only once. And even that was an injustice.

But mud sticks and once you have a reputation in football it never leaves you. It probably makes life easier for journalists. They can recycle the lazy old clichés about Tam Forsyth the hard man. I am not denying that I was a wholehearted player or that my job was to break up attacks. I was committed and I never shirked a tackle in my life. But I can honestly say hand on heart that I never deliberately went over the top or set out to injure another player. The guys I played against were for the most part just like me – honest pros trying to make a living from the game. I would never have dreamt of trying to injure them. It wasn't the way I had been brought up and I could never have lived with myself if someone had been hurt because of a tackle that was contrary to the spirit of the game.

So where did my unwelcome reputation come from?

I believe it all started with the most high-profile fixture of them all. An Old Firm cup final. In this case the League Cup final that was played on Saturday, 25 October 1975.

Quite simply I became a victim of the great Celtic propaganda machine.

As so often happens in finals it was a disappointing game, not helped by the demanding midweek European ties both clubs had just played. Although we had lost three games on the spin, including a European Cup tie to St Etienne, we won the final 1–0 thanks to a towering performance from John Greig and a stunning diving header from wee Alex MacDonald that fairly flew into the net. Most of the pundits took the view that we had deserved our narrow victory in what had been a scrappy, bad-tempered game.

But Celtic did not accept the result with good grace. Sean Fallon was their temporary manager in the absence of Jock Stein, who was recovering from the injuries he had received in a serious car crash. Perhaps the greater responsibility Sean had taken on was too heavy a burden for his shoulders. We had also, just seven months previously, stopped Celtic from making it ten league titles in a row, kicking the feet from under their aura of invincibility. Or maybe – the thought did cross my mind – Fallon was just a bad loser. Whatever the reason he came out of that Hampden dressing room at the end of the game all guns blazing. He complained bitterly about what he described as the 'roughhouse tactics' used by Rangers.[17] Fallon was also furious that the man in the middle, Bill Anderson of East Kilbride, was not one of Scotland's seven official FIFA referees and therefore to his way of thinking did not have the experience necessary to officiate at such an important game. Celtic told the Sunday papers that they intended to make an official complaint to the management committee of the Scottish League.

When Fallon talked about roughhouse tactics he was referring of course to one Tom Forsyth. I had been booked for a foul on Danny McGrain after fifty-seven minutes, and four minutes later I put in a tackle on Kenny Dalglish, the golden boy of the Celtic team. It was perhaps slightly mistimed but it was, I believe, fairly innocuous compared to some of the stuff that was going on around me. I didn't think it deserved another booking and nor did Mr Anderson. He did nothing, much to the disgust of the Celtic players, management team and fans, who wanted me to get a second booking and as a result my marching orders.

The furore about the referee's decision not to send me off had still not calmed down by the time we came back for training on the Monday morning. The papers kept the pot boiling and throughout the week the correspondence columns of the newspapers were full of letters either condemning or defending me. Rangers did not take the criticism from the other side of the city lying down. Big Jock Wallace was furious that I had been portrayed as a dirty player and told the *Glasgow Herald* that: 'If Forsyth ever went over the ball I would tear the head off him. I would stake my life on the fact that he never goes over the ball.' He wasn't just blindly defending one of his players, as managers are inclined to do. Jock was as honest as the day is long and he would never have made a statement like that if he didn't believe it was true. Rangers also took the

---

[17] It is quite ironic that, like me, Fallon was also known as Iron Man during his playing days with Celtic in the 1950s. A hard-tackling, rugged full back who took no prisoners Sean once said 'I was just an ordinary player with a big heart and a fighting spirit to recommend me.'

unusual step of writing to the Scottish League in my defence. The club felt that undue pressure was being put on me, especially with a league game against Celtic to be played just a week after the final (Incidentally, it was said I gave a rather subdued performance in that game, so perhaps the events of the previous Saturday were preying on my mind.)

My own view was quite straightforward. Sometimes decisions will go for you and sometimes they will go against you; these things have a habit of balancing themselves out over the course of a season. You take the rough with the smooth, pick yourself up and move on to the next game. Coming out and slaughtering people in the press after a defeat was anathema to me; it was not how fellow professionals should be treated. I felt that Fallon had run to the papers and put the knife in and that, coming from a fellow professional, disappointed me. What he did not say was that, if anything, Celtic were even guiltier of 'roughhouse' tactics than Rangers. The first four fouls of the game went against the men in green and white, and they also had three men booked, two of them for retaliatory tackles on me. (There was just no pleasing Celtic that day. Fallon was also enraged by these bookings, for Harry Hood and Pat McCluskey, and gave notice that they would support appeals by the players.) One paper also reports that Andy Lynch 'had a go at Forsyth and was lucky the ref did not see him'. But when you are watching from the opposition dugout these are the things you are likely to miss.

What about a neutral point of view? The late Ian Archer – for many years a distinguished sportswriter on the *Glasgow Herald* but not someone you would ever describe as Rangers-minded – argues that my marking of Dalglish had been 'decisive' in Rangers winning the final. More interestingly, he observes that this 'man of iron' is 'hard but not, I think, unsporting. As a person Forsyth is a sportsman, of that I am sure.' While John Fairgrieve – writing in the *Sunday Mail* a week after the final – also absolves me of the charge of unsportsmanlike behaviour. He admits he did not like my style of play, which he found a little too robust, but concludes, 'He is not in my submission a malicious player. He does go for the ball rather than the man.'

As for my one sending-off in the senior game that too was a farce. It was September 1977. We were at Love Street to play St Mirren where my direct opponent was Frank McGarvey, later of Liverpool and Celtic fame. Early in the game Frank caught me with a late challenge and I reacted by pushing him away. More than anything it was a silly reaction on my part but the ref took it upon himself to book me. Later in the proceedings I was bringing the ball out of defence and played a one-two with a teammate. As I ran past my opponent to collect the return pass he body-checked me, taking me out of the play. I made my way back to my defensive position thinking no more about what had happened. But then to my surprise the ref made a beeline for me and said that the linesman had seen me fouling the St Mirren player. I was promptly given my marching orders.

Getting dismissed was bad enough but I now had an even more traumatic encounter to look forward to: with my manager. Sure enough he was apoplectic – hardly surprising as we had drawn 3–3 with a side we were expected to beat. As soon as he walked into the dressing room at full time he confronted me.

'You were a stupid bastard getting sent off. It cost us a win,' he thundered in the confines of the dressing room. I tried to tell him what had really happened but Jock was still seething with emotion and my explanation fell on deaf ears.

There was an even more worrying prospect when I walked into Ibrox for training on the Monday morning.

'The manager wants to see you in his office right away,' I was told.

My heart was in my mouth as I climbed those famous marble stairs. I thought I was either going to be fined or be forced to sit through another bollocking, or both. But when I sat down, Jock, to my relief, had changed his tune.

'Listen son. I watched the highlights of the game yesterday and you shouldn't have been sent off. Sorry I shouted at you in the dressing room but it was done in the heat of the moment.'

That was Jock all over: passionate and committed to the cause but honest enough to own up to a mistake and to apologise for it. That was the mark of the man.

At my disciplinary hearing only one member of the SFA panel took my side, Tom Fagan of Albion Rovers. The rest, to my dismay, voted to confirm the referee's decision. The upshot was I was given a three-week ban. All they had to do was to watch the highlights, as Big Jock had done, and they would have seen that I was the innocent party. But for some obscure reason television evidence was not permissible in those days. That would have been too much like common sense. I have always viewed the people who run the SFA as amateurs – amateurs who sit in judgement on professionals, guys who are trying to make a living from the game. Suspensions ate away at your wages; there was no bonus or appearance money. Worse than that another guy would take your place in the team and if he shone you might be out for a lot longer than the period of suspension.

So my tough-guy reputation, I believe, was broadly speaking a negative. It made me a marked man in the eyes of opposition fans, the media and, most important of all, referees. I have no doubt it contributed significantly to the thirty or so bookings I picked up in my sixteen-year career in the pro game. It also made things more difficult when I did go in front of the beaks. On one occasion, not long after the Dalglish incident, I was due to go in front of the disciplinary committee as I had accumulated three bookings. I was being represented at the hearing by Gordon Dunwoodie of the players' union. But when I arrived at Park Gardens, Gordon let out a long sigh and gave me his considered verdict:

'You've got no chance Tam.'

Gordon, like everyone else, had read about the fuss Celtic had made in the wake of the League Cup final and he knew that would be in the minds of the panel members, no matter how hard they tried to be objective. That is just human nature.

Referees like the rest of us are influenced by the things they read and my reputation as a hard man, which started in my Motherwell days, meant that they would be unlikely to give me the benefit of the doubt. I heard from a reliable source that they used to discuss me at their training sessions.

'Who have you got on Saturday?' one of the whistlers asked his colleague.

'Motherwell versus Hibs at Fir Park,' was the reply.

'Watch that big bastard Forsyth.'

That, I was told, is an accurate account of a conversation that took place at a referees' training session in the west of Scotland. It was no wonder then that while other players would get a ticking off yours truly would be given a booking for the same offence.

The thing is I don't believe my bad reputation was justified. It obviously grated at the time, because for that 'Iron Men' series I told the *Sunday Mail*.

> It all adds up to me being a hatchet-man defender who relies totally on strength and force to stop an opponent. Of course I am a hard player and can use my physique. You need to be in modern football. But I am also a footballer who takes pride in my skill.

I am just grateful that many people in the game saw beyond the image that the media had so carefully cultivated. For those same 'Iron Men' articles Jock Wallace said that while I gave the team much-needed power and aggression I also had the 'polish and style to go with [my] other attributes'. You would perhaps expect my club manager to say something like that but when opponents voice similar sentiments it speaks volumes. In January 1975 Davie Hay of Celtic wrote an article for the *Daily Record* in which he assessed the Rangers players prior to an Old Firm league clash at Ibrox. Davie was kind enough to give me eight out of ten, with only Sandy Jardine (nine) getting a higher rating. He was also quite complimentary about my abilities as a footballer.

> He is a vital player to Rangers back four. You can see the trouble they have when he is out of the side. He played in midfield and this helps him in his distribution, which is excellent.

Many journalists saw beyond the one-dimensional portrayal. Even John Fairgrieve, a critic of my style of play, thought that, 'He has a lot more skill than he permits himself to show.' While I was still at Motherwell another paper noted that Bobby Howitt had moved me from central defence into midfield because of my 'close-in dribbling skills and deceptive long stride'. And Hugh Taylor – admittedly a bluenose but an eminent and respected writer on a range of Scottish papers – gave the following opinion after a Scotland–England clash: 'Who said Forsyth can't play. There's class as well as power in Big Tam's play.'

Speaking of international football I just don't think I would have won twenty-two Scotland caps or played in the World Cup finals if I had been nothing more than a hard man. The game at that level asks searching questions of players and you couldn't possibly play against the likes of Brazil, Argentina, Holland or England without a fair degree of skill and technique.

I also got some backing from the most unlikely of sources: a referee. When highly respected whistler John Paterson retired after seventeen years at the top level (he also handled big matches for both FIFA and UEFA) he said that players 'like Tom Forsyth' never bothered him. That was because, in his view, we were strong and honest, as opposed to the guys he really didn't like, the 'nigglers and cheats'. Well said Mr Paterson.

I would never claim to have even a fraction of the skill that the Davie Coopers, Paul Gascoignes and Brian Laudrups of this world had. Those guys were geniuses who were worth the admission money on their own. In terms of technical ability I wasn't in their league. My overriding strengths were power, determination and a will to win. But nor was I simply a bruiser.

I like to think I had a bit more about me than that.

10

The First Treble

The League Cup triumph in October meant that we were now the only side that could win the treble for season 1975/76. It was no longer a pipe dream; after all we were now the reigning league champions and the confidence that gives you is incredible. We expected to win every time we played and if our standards ever dropped, even for just part of a game, we knew that Big Jock would be on our case right away. He was the complete perfectionist.

It helped that our key players were firing on all cylinders. None more so than big Derek Johnstone. He was something of an enigma: he seemed to hate training with a passion and to prefer playing at centre half (which I thought was another example of his desire for an easy life), but he was one hell of a goal scorer. I think he got twenty-eight for us that season, many from midfield, which was just as well because our recognised strikers didn't contribute all that much. Jock tried Colin Stein, Derek Parlane and young Martin Henderson up front but it didn't happen for any of them, at least not on a consistent basis. In our league games they scored a grand total of sixteen goals between them, with Martin by far the most prolific. DJ was simply immense, a fact recognised by Jock Wallace, who described him at the time as the best player in Britain. I don't know about that but Johnstone had two good feet and was by some distance the best header of a ball I have ever seen; he seemed to climb higher than anyone else, and when he was up there he rarely put his headers anywhere but on target.

Our midfield was quite exceptional. Bobby McKean, Tommy McLean and Alex MacDonald hardly missed a game all season, giving the team solidity and consistency of performance. If I had to pick out one guy from our engine room it would be Alex MacDonald; 'Wee Doddy' was a revelation, winning innumerable player-of-the-year awards from our supporters. The phrase box-to-box midfielder could have been invented for him because the way he got up and down that park was simply incredible. But the strongest unit in the team was the defence, which for the most part was big Peter McCloy in goal and a back four of Jardine, Forsyth, Jackson and Greig. In thirty-four league games we conceded a miserly twenty-four goals, compared to the forty-two our nearest challengers, Celtic, let in.

I don't think you would have found a stronger pair of full-backs anywhere in the world and I do not make that claim lightly. They were both sensational, although Sandy did miss quite a few games through injury. It came as no surprise to anyone when Greigy was named player of the year by the Scottish Football Writers' Association for 1976, which meant the award stayed at Ibrox, as Sandy won it in 1975. For my own part I was now a regular at centre back, my favoured position, where I was deployed alongside Colin Jackson. We complemented each other perfectly, given his prowess in the air and mine in the tackle, and despite his often incomprehensible Aberdonian accent we soon forged an excellent understanding. And if we did falter there was big Peter McCloy, the Girvan Lighthouse, to get us out of jail. Peter proved all-season long just how good a keeper he was.

However, we were disappointed by our form in the league during the first half of the season. Despite an opening-day victory at Ibrox over Celtic there were some defeats that have to be filed under embarrassing, including a 3–0 defeat to Ayr United at Somerset Park in October, followed a week later by another away defeat, this time to Motherwell, while in November we lost to both Edinburgh clubs.

I can only put those lapses down to our demanding schedule. To win the League Cup we had to play ten games between August and October, including that emotional roller-coaster of a final against our

Old Firm rivals. Then there was the little matter of the European Cup. In the first round we were drawn against Bohemians from the Republic of Ireland. For once the talk going into a European tie was not about the football, but about the possibility of trouble off the field. At the time the Troubles in Northern Ireland were at their peak, and, given the sympathies of the two sets of supporters, there was certainly potential for violence. It never really materialised, which I think was largely due to our performance in the first leg in Glasgow. We tore the Irishmen apart, with Derek Johnstone grabbing two goals in a 4–1 win. It meant the second leg in Dublin was little more than a formality, which I think took a lot of the heat out of the game and the occasion. So despite a tenser than normal atmosphere inside the ground and a few skirmishes between the Rangers and Bohemians fans the game – which finished one apiece – passed off without too much rancour.

It was to be a different story in round two, where we were drawn against French champions St Etienne. It was a difficult draw but to be honest when it was made we rather fancied our chances. Football in France was probably not as strong as it is now and, after all, at that time, no French club had ever won a European trophy. Rangers also had a good record against Gallic opposition, having knocked St Etienne out of the European Cup in 1957 and Rennes out of the European Cup Winners Cup in 1971/72. Our only reverse was against Nice in the club's first-ever foray into the European Cup in 1956/57, when Rangers lost a third attempt to settle the tie at the neutral Parc de Princes in Paris after both teams had won their home legs 2–1.

If further incentive was needed to win the tie it was the venue for the final: Hampden Park. What a night that would be for our fans. Sadly, the two legs against the champions of France were little short of disastrous. The fact is that St Etienne had a wonderful team at that time, and an excellent young manager in Robert Herbin, a highly successful former player. The shining star was Dominique Rocheteau, the so-called 'Green Angel', who was a very quick and skilful outside right and one of the best players that France has ever produced. He won three titles with St Etienne and played in the France team that was victorious in the European Championships of 1984, alongside the likes of Platini, Giresse and Tigana. St Etienne were far from a one-man team and they were particularly dangerous up front thanks to the brothers Revelli, Patrick and Herve.

The first leg was on 22 October 1975, just three days before we were due to face Celtic in *that* League Cup final. There was a disaster even before the game started. As we were warming up in the Guichard stadium big Peter McCloy damaged his wrist and was ruled out of the game, his place being taken by Stewart Kennedy. Worse was to follow. The home side completely dominated the opening stages with their fast, attacking football, pinning us back in our own half. Given the barrage we were under it was perhaps surprising that it took them twenty-five minutes to open the scoring, through Patrick Revelli. After that, ever so gradually, we managed to claw our way back into the game and as the ninety minutes drew to a close we felt that with only a single-goal deficit to contend with we could have our say at Ibrox in the return.

Then the roof fell in. With just seconds remaining and the referee looking at his watch we shot ourselves well and truly in the foot. Wee Doddy, normally so reliable, played a loose pass across his own penalty area. It was intercepted by another of their excellent players, Dominique Bathenay, and he rifled the ball past Stewart to give them a 2–0 win.

Reversing a two-goal deficit against a team of their calibre was a tall order for anyone and although we gave it our all at Ibrox a fortnight later they once again showed their class. Strikes from Herve Revelli and Rocheteau made the tie safe for St Etienne and our only consolation was a goal from Alex MacDonald in the last minute. While I am sure it made Doddy feel better about himself after the mistake in France we trudged disconsolately off the pitch after being eliminated 4–1 on aggregate. As every football fan will know St Etienne were a lot better than some people gave them credit for and they knocked out Dynamo Kiev and PSV Eindhoven on the way to the final at Hampden, where they lost 1–0 to Bayern Munich.

Despite the disappointment at going out of the competition there was real respect and genuine warmth between the two clubs. St Etienne's manager said that the Rangers people were the friendliest he had ever met in football and he even named his two cocker spaniels Glasgow and Rangers! When the final did come around, in May 1976, the visiting French fans got a warm welcome from Rangers fans, despite the fact they played in a green strip and were nicknamed *les verts* (the greens). Rangers even gave them Ibrox to train on as they prepared to meet Bayern.

They say that every cloud has a silver lining and our exit from the European Cup proved that there is some truth in that old cliché. We could now concentrate on the premier league[18] and after a sticky few weeks our form was exceptional. In fact after losing by a single goal to Aberdeen at Pittodrie on 6 December we went undefeated in the league until the end of the season; a twenty-one-game unbeaten run, twenty-six if you include the Scottish Cup. The clincher came at Tannadice on 24 April 1976. We not only secured the championship with our 1–0 win but also the goal, from Derek Johnstone after just twenty-two seconds, was the fastest ever scored by Rangers (little did we know that big Derek would break even that record before the season was out). It was so early in the game that half of our travelling support was not even in the ground.

We ended the campaign with a comfortable six-point lead over Celtic. For me it meant a second league-winner's medal to add to my League Cup and Scottish Cup badges. My personal silverware count was rising and I couldn't have been happier. But there was still time for one last hurrah. By the time the Scottish Cup came around our form was quite exceptional and we carried it into that competition. In the earlier rounds the highlight was undoubtedly the 4–1 win over Aberdeen on 14 February, a real St Valentine's Day massacre. There were 60,000 at Ibrox that afternoon, our second-biggest home crowd of the season and boy did we give them value for money. We then trounced Queen of the South by five goals to nil at Palmerston and beat Motherwell 3–2 at Hampden in the semi-final.

Our opponents in the final were Hearts, and a crowd of 85,354

---

[18] It was the inaugural season of the premier league, with the top division reduced to ten teams, playing each other four times. The new set-up was criticised by some but being the first team to win the title under the new rules made it even more special.

rolled up to Hampden to see if we could clinch the treble. To be honest we won easily and dominated proceedings from start to finish. Big DJ broke another record for the earliest goal when he notched the opener after forty-two seconds, latching onto an exquisite free kick from Tommy McLean. It was further into the game than his title-clincher at Dundee United but because the ref got proceedings under way slightly early it was actually scored before the official starting time of three o'clock. The whole team played well that day but I have to pay a special tribute to John Greig. Although he was nearing the end of his playing career and had been plagued by injuries he was magnificent. Playing in midfield he drove the team on, leading as he always did by example. It must have been so special for him, captaining this great club to its first treble since 1963/64; a team that he also graced. He was such an inspiration to every Rangers player and there was just no way you could let your standards drop when he was in the side.

As we celebrated that night I was the happiest man alive. Winning trophies with a club like Rangers is a real honour; winning a treble is special. I knew that our fans all over the world – and they are all over the world – would also be in party mode. The league triumph the season before could perhaps be dismissed as a one-off, perhaps even as a flash in the pan. But to win a treble puts the question of who is the best beyond all doubt. Bluenoses everywhere now had all the bragging rights they could ever wish for.

There was another good reason for my joy. The team had played consistently well all season, but so had I. It was undoubtedly my best campaign as a professional footballer and what's more people were beginning to sit up and take notice. I have to admit, however, that I did have one dodgy day and it came against Hearts at Tynecastle on 3 January 1976. After seventy-one minutes I was trying to clear a deep cross into the area but only succeeded in heading the ball past Peter McCloy. I don't know who was more surprised, me or him. I didn't know where to look and I just slumped to the ground in despair at what I had done. It was a beautifully executed header, of the type, notes the *Sunday Mail*, 'normally associated with Denis Law'. Although we ran out winners Big Jock was not best pleased and he tore strips off me in the dressing room at the end of the game.

That little mishap aside I was delighted with the contribution I had made. And as I said it did not go unnoticed. In another league game against Hearts, this time at Ibrox, Allan Herron was highly complimentary in the *Sunday Mail*, even praising my playmaking skills:

> Love him or hate him this was Tom Forsyth's greatest game in a Rangers strip. He broke brilliantly with the ball, hit some superb passes and was always in the right place at the right time. The match certainly showed up the full potential of this iron man, who is so often the victim of unjust criticism from those who have to face him.

Then after we had beaten Hibs by three goals to nil at Easter Road on 3 April 1976, Dixon Blackstock was also generous with his praise:

> The man who led the charge was the guy the opposition fans love to hate – big Tom Forsyth. Not only did Tiger Tom take care of his job in defence he took time to go goal hunting as well. It was a typical Forsyth charge upfield that brought the second Rangers goal. He brushed Brownlie aside to win the ball, forced his way to the byeline and squared for Martin Henderson to blast home a great left-foot drive.

There were quite a few similar reports in the papers during 1975/76. I felt that after nine years in the professional game I had been invited to the top table. All that was needed to make things perfect was a call-up from my country. After a few false starts with the national team I felt that I was ready to play my part on the biggest stage of all.

Although I could never have predicted the storm that was to follow.

11

Life in Light Blue

Having been around Scottish football my whole life I knew of course that Rangers were a big club. But when I walked through the front door for my first day of training the sheer size of the place still took my breath away. Everything was massive: the stands, the dressing rooms, even the offices. You could easily get lost inside Ibrox, not something that was a problem at Fir Park. Despite working there every day I often had to pinch myself to make sure it wasn't a dream. At the same time there were new rules to learn. Players were expected to turn up on time for training on time – and woe-betide those who didn't – and to wear a collar and tie when reporting for work. It was a disciplined, professional environment, something that was reflected in the character of our manager, Jock Wallace, who carried himself like the professional soldier he once was.[19]

You can't help but be affected by the grandeur of Ibrox or by the club's proud history and glorious traditions. I thought about the men who had come before, especially the defensive titans like Davie Meiklejohn, Willie Woodburn, Sammy Cox, George Young and of course my new teammate, John Greig. Legends all; I knew that I had much to live up to. The fortunes of Rangers will always fluctuate, from year to year

---

[19] Jock served for three years with the King's Own Scottish Borderers.

and decade to decade, but these are temporary phenomena. For me it is the greatest club on the planet and it always will be.

It is of course inevitable that expectations at Ibrox are incredibly high, stratospheric even. You wouldn't want it any other way. It does bring its own unique pressures. You are expected to win every game – and I do mean every game – while playing attractive, attacking football. Some people, good players in their own right, find the pressure to succeed too much of a burden and fall by the wayside. Others, however, thrive and are spurred on by the intensity of life in the Ibrox hothouse.

I got a taste of what was expected early in my Rangers career. Although strangely enough it was the result of a performance I gave in the dark blue of Scotland rather than in the light blue of Rangers. I had been part of the team that played Northern Ireland in the 1976 home internationals. Having got changed after the match I made my way out of the stadium, and happy that we had won the game I walked through the front door at Hampden.

My reverie was rudely interrupted. Out of the corner of my eye I spotted a figure striding purposefully towards me.

It was Willie Waddell.

He cornered me just outside the main entrance and gave me a piece of his mind.

'It is unacceptable for a Rangers player to perform so badly when representing Scotland,' he barked.

I was stunned, lost for words. I thought he might have been joking but I could see in his eyes that he was deadly serious. To me, that epitomised Waddell – a man who had given his all for Rangers as a player, manager and executive and expected the rest of us to do the same. Jock Wallace was exactly the same. To him and Waddell, Rangers was a cause, a way of life, and you either had to shape up or ship out.

It wasn't just Waddell who would be critical of your performances. I remember one time we were playing Hibs at Ibrox in a Scottish Cup tie in 1973 and winning 1–0. Then, at a corner, I was meant to be marking Alan Gordon but managed to lose him. Just my luck; he got his head to the ball and scored with a powerful header. There was no more scoring and we walked off the pitch with a 1–1 draw and facing a tough replay at Easter Road. Jock Wallace was not a happy camper.

As soon as I got into the dressing room he gave me a real tongue-lashing. But that was Jock. He was so committed, so passionate, so Rangers; he just couldn't help himself. You understood what drove him and waited till the storm passed.

You got a good idea of what was expected of Rangers players during Jock's training sessions. It was much more rigorous than anything I had experienced at Motherwell. There was more emphasis on running, fitness and building up your body strength. While there was of course ball work and practice games my abiding memory is of pounding round the running track at Ibrox or circuit training in the gym. It was hard going but you definitely got fitter, something that is essential at a club like Rangers, where you take part in so many high-intensity games. It must have been a real shock to my system because just after joining up at Ibrox I was out for eight weeks due to a hamstring injury I picked up in training.

Jock Wallace was a very methodical man. He very rarely varied the training routines, something that also applied to our pre-season sessions on Gullane beach, which is in East Lothian. Jock would start you off on a gently sloping sand dune, then we moved to a steeper one and then on to an even steeper one until we came to the mound known (rightly) as 'Murder Hill'. Our time at Gullane was so physically demanding that sometimes you got the dry 'boak', as they call it in this part of the world. Surprisingly perhaps we preferred the Gullane sessions to running round the track at Ibrox, which was just so monotonous. Many pundits had a right good laugh about us running up and down those sand dunes but if you look at Jock's record you would have to say he had the last laugh. We were rarely found wanting when it came to the business end of the season.

Despite the rigours of Jock's training regime there wasn't much in the way of what today would be called sports science. We had a fitness coach and a masseur but there was no measuring of our cardiovascular health or anything like that. Nor did we get any advice on diet. I was a big eater in those days and regularly tucked into chips, bread and red meat, all the things that the player of today is told to avoid. My worst habit however was the weed. I smoked between twenty and thirty fags a day, which would also be anathema to the modern-day manager,

although I can honestly say it didn't have any effect on my performances. It was a habit I picked up at school and one I carried on
throughout my playing career.

Although teams were not as obsessed about tactics and formations
in those days there was certainly more emphasis on them than at
Motherwell. In the dressing room before a game Jock would get his
blackboard out and go over what we had discussed earlier in the week.
It may not sound that much but it was more than either Ally MacLeod
or Willie Ormond did when I played for Scotland. But it was on the
motivational side that Jock really stood out. He would tell you how
good you were, that you were better than your immediate opponent;
that victory was assured if you gave 100 per cent. Then just before
you were about to run down the tunnel he would say: 'Don't let me
down. Don't let Rangers down.' By the time you got onto that pitch
you would have run through a brick wall for the man.

The other big change about playing for Rangers was the strong
desire of every team we came up against to beat us. It was the other
side of the coin for me. I had felt the same way about beating Rangers
(and Celtic) when I was at Motherwell and I could understand that
mentality. I think there are two reasons for players being so fired up
when they face the Old Firm. In most years it is likely that they will
be playing the current champions when they play Rangers or Celtic and
players the world over want to beat the best. Secondly, most players are
desperate to play for one of the Old Firm clubs – I know I was – and feel
that a good performance against them will help secure that coveted big-
money transfer. So it might be the most well-worn cliché of all time but
there really are no easy games for either Rangers or Celtic in Scotland.

A great example of what I am talking about is the Ayr United team
of the 1970s. When you faced them at Somerset – a crumbling, atmos-
pheric old stadium where the crowd is practically on top of the players
– you knew there would be no quarter either asked for or granted.
Under their greatest ever manager, Ally MacLeod – an undoubted success in club football, despite his inadequacies with Scotland – the Honest
Men ran through metaphorical brick walls every time we went down
to the seaside. Roared on by crowds that were often in excess of fifteen
thousand, every fifty-fifty ball was a matter of life and death.

Ayr had some great players in those days. Guys like Dick Malone, John 'Spud' Murphy, Stan 'The Mighty' Quinn and a certain Alex Ferguson. But I will always remember my clashes with their tough-as-teak centre forward Alex 'Dixie' Ingram. He acquired the Dixie moniker thanks to his prowess in the air but to me his greatest quality was his courage. This guy would have put his head in front of an Exocet missile and I think the Ayr trainer lost count of the number of times Dixie was taken off with a head knock or a bloody nose. Our duels were so fierce that I expected to see the ball being carried off on a stretcher at full time. After facing him you thought of the famous quotation: 'football is a game for gentlemen played by hooligans'.

One mid-week, after we had played Ayr on the Saturday, I was strolling though Motherwell town centre when a suave, sophisticated man dressed in a smart business suit, called out to me:

'How are you today, Mr Forsyth?'

I thought: 'It can't be . . . can it?'

But yes, it was indeed Dixie Ingram, the man who had spent a whole afternoon roughing me up. He was on the way to his day job as an executive in the motor trade, an industry in which he would achieve great success when his football career ended. I don't think I have ever met anyone off the field who was so different to his on-field persona.

Apart from the fact that teams always seemed to raise their game when they played Rangers another problem we had was the quality of the opposition. Elsewhere in this book I talk about the great players Celtic had in the 1970s and early 1980s but every team we faced had genuine class. Hibs had guys like Pat Stanton, Alex Cropley, John Blackley, John Brownlie and Arthur Duncan. Aberdeen had men of the calibre of Joe Harper, Drew Jarvie, Willie Miller, Alex McLeish, Gordon Strachan, Jim Leighton and many others besides. Dundee United could field David Narey, Paul Sturrock, Andy Gray and Paul Hegarty. St Mirren's roster included Frank McGarvey, Tony Fitzpatrick and Lex Richardson. And what about Andy Ritchie of Morton, Donald Ford of Hearts, Henry Hall of St Johnstone, Alan Rough of Partick Thistle and Willie Pettigrew of Motherwell. These boys could all hack it at the highest level and – what a contrast with today – they were all Scottish.

Another problem that I – and indeed all Old Firm players of the time – had to deal with was the attitude of the SFA when it came to disciplinary matters. I remember one time I was up in front of the disciplinary committee, having accumulated three bookings. Also on the carpet that day were my fellow miscreants: Davie Hay of Celtic and Gordon McQueen, who was then a young, up-and-coming player at St Mirren. Both guys, like me, had three bookings to answer for. I think the committee had twelve members, the vast majority from clubs like Stranraer, Brechin City and Queen of the South. There was no set penalty for three bookings in those days; it was purely at the discretion of the committee whether you got a suspension or a fine, or indeed both.

You can probably guess what happened.

Davie Hay and I both got suspended (for four days) and we also got fined £20 each. Big Gordon walked out of Park Gardens with a severe censure, which he must have thought was a real result. It seemed to me there was one rule for the Old Firm and one for every other club.

The other thing that used to annoy me in my playing days was the way that some referees treated you with a distinct lack of respect. All that jabbing and wagging of fingers when they wanted to give you a talking to. There was no need for it. A bit of common courtesy would have gone a long way in building up our respect for the men in black. Sometimes, however, they picked on the wrong player and got more than they bargained for. I remember an incident involving Willie Johnston at Ibrox, which I think occurred during his second spell at Rangers. Bud had been fouled by a defender but managed to keep his balance and ploughed on regardless. But the referee didn't play the advantage and whistled for a foul. Willie wasn't a happy camper and remonstrated with the ref. The official, no doubt aware of Bud's chequered disciplinary record, pointed his finger at him and then wagged it vigorously, indicating that Bud should come over for a lecture.

He got the shock of his life when Bud refused to move.

I think by that point, angered by the initial decision and the subsequent use of the finger, Willie had completely lost the plot and wasn't about to do anything to help this particular man in black. The more that hapless ref pointed and gestured at Willie the more determined he was to stay put. And stay put he did. In the end the ref bottled it, and

Playing for Scotland. I was always so proud to pull on that dark-blue jersey and represent my country.

Clearing the ball in the England–Scotland clash at Wembley in 1977, watched by Mick Channon.

Scotland–England at Hampden, 1978.
(*courtesy Colorsport*)

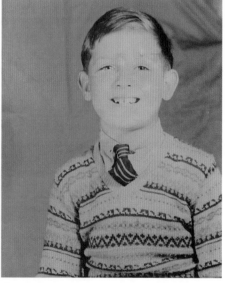

Early days. (*Clockwise, from top*)
My father, David; My mother,
Anne, and dad getting married;
me as a schoolboy at Stonehouse
primary; with my twin brother
Robert, my sister Margaret and my
mother in Paisley town centre; dad,
who worked for a time in farming,
with a fine Clydesdale horse.

I was a mascot for Stonehouse Amateurs and this is me with two cups won by the team.

It might only have been a young farmers' competition but it was still my first trophy! Playing for Hamilton and District Young Farmers we won the West Area Young Farmers title. (*I am front row, middle*)

In 1967, at the age of eighteen, I travelled to London with Glenavon Amateurs. We played Crystal Palace colts at Selhurst Park and beat them 5–1. There was an even bigger thrill the next day when we went to Wembley to see Scotland beat world champions England 3–2. (*I am on the far left*)

With my pals Tam Campbell (sitting next to me) and Billy Paterson.

Family man

Arran was always a favourite holiday destination for the Forsyth family and here I am with (*from left*) Julie, David and Karen.

Linda and I on holiday in Majorca, 1974.

My three children: Karen, David and Julie.

I was delighted to sign for Motherwell in 1967 because I had supported the team as a boy, inspired by the famous 'Ancell Babes'. Here I am in that famous claret-and-amber in a game against Rangers at Fir Park helping our keeper, the great Peter McCloy. The Rangers players are Colin Stein (left) and Willie Johnston.

With my Scotland teammates in Moscow, 1971 prior to an international match with the Soviet Union. I was still at Motherwell then. The building in the centre of the photo is the famous Bolshoi theatre. (*From left to right*) Colin Stein, Bobby Clark, Keith MacRae, Bobby Watson and me.

We enjoyed some great tussles with the Old Firm, especially at Fir Park. In this game with Celtic I have obviously been agitated by something and am being held back by teammate Jimmy Wilson. The player remonstrating with the referee is our captain, Bobby Campbell, and the other Motherwell player is John Goldthorpe. The three Celtic players are (*from left*) Bertie Auld, John Hughes and John Clark.

Motherwell, circa 1969, in our 'Real Madrid' strip! Back row (*from left*) Whiteford, Wark, Forsyth, McCloy, W. McCallum, B. Campbell.
Front (*from left*) Wilson, Donnelly, Deans, McInally, Muir, J. Murray

Becoming a Ranger. Linda and I in October 1972, just after I signed my contract at Ibrox. The papers sent a photographer to our house.

With the late, great Davie Cooper, the most skilful player I ever played with or against.

The centenary Scottish Cup final 1973 and *that* goal.

Derek Johnstone's header had hit the post and rolled along the goal line. I limber up to put the ball away.

Sticking it away.

It's time to celebrate!

That goal in the 1973 final was my first for Rangers and how I celebrated.

Lifting the Cup. DJ looks on as I hold up the Scottish Cup.

The Old Firm experience. Games against Celtic were invariably the highlight of the domestic season. Here I am straining every sinew to protect our goal, watched by teammates (*from left to right*) Sandy Jardine, Stewart Kennedy, Colin Jackson and Willie Mathieson.

My last medal. The 1981 Scottish Cup final would be ninth and last major honour with Rangers.

A special match was arranged at Stonehouse bowling club, of which I have long been a member, as part of my Rangers testimonial. Here I am with (*from left to right*) Sandy Jardine, Peter McCloy and Colin 'Bomber' Jackson.

Captain of Scotland. I played for Scotland twenty-two times but only captained the team once, in this match against Switzerland. Leading out the team (*above*). In the thick of the action (*below*)

We wore it well. Rod Stewart popped into our training camp at Dunblane in the run-up to the 1978 World Cup in Argentina to wish us all the best. I am in the middle of a group that comprised (*from left to right*) Gordon McQueen, Joe Jordan, Rod and Kenny Dalglish.

Scotland on tour in South America, 1977. This is how we lined up before a game with Argentina, in the course of which some of their players completely lost the plot. I am in the front row, on the far right.

Management

I had ten great years as assistant to Tommy McLean at Fir Park. In our first season at Fir Park we guided the club back to the premier league and I am shown here with (*from left*) reserve-ream coach Cammy Murray, Tommy and the trophy for winning the first-division title.

With Tommy outside Fir Park

At work and play

Bowling is my other sport and I have been a keen player for more than forty years. This is the Stonehouse bowling-club rink at Northfield in Ayr for the 1996 Scottish national championships, for which we had qualified by winning our district final. The other member of the rink were (*from left to right*) Hugh Smith, Jim Robertson, the skip, and Jim Wallace.

I have always been a keen gardener, something that I inherited from my father. This is a petunia I grew in my greenhouse.

I work in corporate hospitality for Rangers on match-days. It is great that I am able to work alongside so many of my boyhood heroes. Colin Jackson is alongside me in the back row and at the front are (*from left to right*) Eric Caldow, Willie Henderson, the late, great Jim Baxter, Ralph Brand and Davie Wilson. What would that lot be worth today?

(*Above*) The Forsyths. Linda and I have quite a family these days.

Back row: daughter-in-law Diane, son David, daughter Karen, my wife Linda, yours truly, daughter Julie and son-in-law Dean

Middle row: Grand-daughter Sophie (8), father-in-law Tom Barr, mother-in-law Agnes Barr and grand-daughter Emma (7)

Front row: My three grand-sons: Mason (7), Max (2) and Cammy (5)

(*Right*) My three children, (*from left*) Julie, David and Karen

took no action. I had no sympathy for the official. If he had been more respectful there would have been no bust up and it could all have been put to bed with a quiet word in Bud's ear.

Having said that, there were some very able referees around in my day. The late, great Tom 'Tiny' Wharton OBE was the pick of the bunch. Tiny, who was six-foot-four, oozed authority and was looked up to by players of all clubs. There was no wagging or jabbing of fingers to call you over for a talking-to. That wasn't his style. He treated people with respect and always accorded you the title of 'Mr'.

'Another foul Mr Forsyth and you're in the book,' he would say.

Tom Wharton was not only very tall but also very bulky, which meant that he did not get up and down the park very much. Instead he prowled the area around the centre circle, relying on his linesmen to patrol the distant reaches of the pitch. It worked. He was our top referee for many years, officiating at many international matches, and was later honoured with a gold medal by FIFA for his services to the refereeing profession.

Tiny had a wonderful dry sense of humour and used it to great effect. One of my favourite stories concerns John Lambie, who was playing for Falkirk against Rangers. Falkirk were leading 1–0 and John decided to wind up his opposite number, Davie Wilson.

'We've got you today wee man,' John crowed to Davie.

But John's words were no sooner out of his mouth than Rangers equalised. Then with ten minutes to go Davie burst into the box and was tackled by Lambie. Tiny immediately pointed to the spot.

'But I never touched him ref,' John protested.

'Read the *Sunday Post* tomorrow morning, Mr Lambie,' was Tiny's immediate riposte.

My other notable Tiny anecdote is about Johnny Hamilton, a spirited but argumentative Hearts player of the 1960s, who actually hailed from Larkhall. Johnny had lost his teeth and relied on a full set of falsers, which of course had to be left in the dressing room during games. In the course of this particular match Johnny had his name taken early on and then later in the game committed a second bookable offence. He trudged disconsolately over to where Tiny was standing and heard the great man utter the immortal words:

'The time has come Mr Hamilton for you to rejoin your teeth.'[20]

* * *

Along with the grandeur and the expectations there was also what you might call a very formal, hierarchical atmosphere at Ibrox. I think that went back to Bill Struth's time as manager, when players were expected to wear bowler hats and starched collars and to behave at all times in a manner that reflected the dignity of the club. In my time players were still expected to know their place, as were the wives and girlfriends. For home games the players arrived at Ibrox at noon. I would meet Peter McCloy outside but we then had to leave the girls in the car while we went inside for a pre-match meal. My wife Linda and Anne McCloy would have to wait in the car until two o' clock when the gates opened for the fans and only then would they be allowed entry into the stadium. I think that some provision could have been made for them. After all, they were there to support their husbands and the club. It is different now of course. There is a family lounge, which the players' wives and their children can use, something that was unheard of in my day.

Talking of children, there has also been a real sea change in the way that maternity issues are handled. Due to football commitments I wasn't able to spend the time I would have liked with Linda prior to, and during, the birth of our three children. Karen, our oldest, was born on the morning of Sunday, 9 September 1973 but the day before, while Linda was in labour, I was playing in a league game against Partick Thistle and I had to rush to the hospital in Lanark after the game. I can tell you I never got bathed and changed so quickly in my life. Unlike today you didn't get time off to attend the birth of your children at Rangers, nor at any other club for that matter. It is so different in 2010; players now see it as a right, something I am not going to argue with as family should always come first.

* * *

---

[20] The Hamilton story is taken from Bob Crampsey's obituary of Tiny Wharton, published in *The Scotsman* in July 2005.

The other thing that has never left me from my days at Ibrox is the strength of feeling that Rangers supporters have for the club. It didn't surprise me when two-hundred-thousand fans travelled down to Manchester for the UEFA Cup final because I have long experience of their passion for everything light blue.

I like to think that we reciprocated the backing we got from our support. I attended many functions at supporters clubs during the course of a season, as did all of my teammates. While Jock Wallace encouraged us to go – and more often than not came with us – we didn't have to be asked twice. In fact I considered it a great honour to be invited to so many events. I remember flying up to Wick and across the Irish Sea to Belfast to attend functions.

With the influx of foreign players into the Scottish game it seems to be much harder now for fans to get stars to come along to their nights. Players from abroad do not have the same close relationship with the fans and I often meet bluenoses who bemoan the fact that no one from Ibrox is willing to attend functions.

One year I won a string of player-of-the-year awards from Rangers supporters clubs and in consequence was invited to attend functions and be presented with a trophy. There were so many in fact that on this particular night I agreed to attend three functions, just so that I wouldn't let anyone down. My first port of call that Saturday evening was Paisley and after the presentation ceremony and a quick Q and A I drove to Linwood, just along the road, for the next one. My third stop was in Coatbridge (yes Coatbridge!) where I arrived about quarter past eleven, a little later than I had anticipated. It was a hot summer night and the back door of the supporters club had been left open. As I walked up to the door I heard a loud voice exclaiming:

'The big bastard isn't coming.'

'The big bastard's here,' I replied as I walked into the club.

They were always very enjoyable nights. The Rangers fans were delighted that we had made the effort and they treated us like royalty. After the speeches were made, the toasts drunk and the awards presented there was invariably a sing song and a dance.

Great days.

12

Bad Medicine: My Spat with the Doc

I was delighted – and if I am honest a bit relieved – to be included in the squad for the 1976 home internationals. Thanks to my good form with Rangers I had already played for Scotland that year in a friendly, on 7 April at Hampden, against Switzerland. In fact I was named captain for the match, a huge honour for someone winning only his third full cap. I played reasonably well against the Swiss and even helped to make the only goal of the game after a neat interchange of passes with Kenny Dalglish led to a finish from Willie Pettigrew. But I wasn't kidding myself. The squad had been badly depleted by call-offs, which meant that manager Willie Ormond brought in guys who had been playing well for their clubs and deserved a chance to show what they could do at international level, such as Willie McVie of Motherwell and Bobby McKean of Rangers.

So it was a great thrill when the squad was announced and yours truly was part of it. With three games in nine days, all of them at Hampden, I had a great chance to show the manager that I was worth a regular place in the side. If that is I was lucky enough to be selected. In fact I started all three games. The first was against Wales, in which I played alongside my Rangers defensive partner Colin Jackson. The most notable thing for me wasn't our comfortable 3–1 victory but the fact we had two world-class strikers warming the bench – Kenny Dalglish and Derek Johnstone. That was followed by an impressive win over Northern Ireland: we won 3–0 but it could easily have been more. We ran them ragged, prompting the chant of 'Why are we so good?' from the Tartan Army. It left us in pole position for the title of champions of Britain. All we had to do was to beat England.

The mood in the camp as we prepared to face the English was one of grim determination. They had trounced us by five goals to one at Wembley in the corresponding fixture in 1975 and another loss, especially on that scale, would have been unthinkable. Fans under the age of thirty will hardly be aware of the annual game with the Auld Enemy but in my time it was massive – for both sides. Most Scottish players, me included, would have walked over broken glass to play in it.

In fact the massive importance of the game with England resulted in the biggest controversy of my career and made me angrier than I have ever been, before or since.

In the week leading up to the game Willie Ormond had a decision to make: whether to play me or Martin Buchan as sweeper alongside big Colin Jackson in the centre of defence. I felt I had done nothing wrong against either Wales or Northern Ireland and that my experience of playing alongside Bomber would stand me in good stead. I also reflected on the relationship between Buchan and Willie Ormond, after their bust-up at Wembley the year before. When Buchan was named on the subs' bench he took umbrage and decided to watch the game from the stand, prompting Ormond to observe ruefully that 'Martin really is a law unto himself'. That I felt would work in my favour and taking everything into account I was quietly confident that I would be given the nod.

Then Tommy Docherty opened his big mouth.

Docherty was Buchan's club manager at Manchester United. He was obviously keen for his player to be selected for such an important match and as managers have done since time immemorial he made his views known to the media. Fair enough but it was what he actually said that caused the problem.

'It's like comparing a Clydesdale to a thoroughbred,' Docherty told the assembled press pack. And he didn't mean that Tam Forsyth was the thoroughbred!

His remarks caused a furore. Despite the fact that the European

Cup final between Bayern Munich and St Etienne was being staged in Glasgow that same week the papers had a field day. After all he had trashed an Old Firm player who had just won a treble in the run-up to the biggest match in the sporting calendar. Rangers fans were livid and the fact that Docherty had once been a Celtic player did not help his cause with them either. When I read what he had said I did my best to stay calm but inside I was seething with anger. Criticism was something I could handle but I felt he had gone out of his way to humiliate me. At that moment I made a vow to prove him wrong, no matter what I had to do. I would show Mr Tommy Docherty.

It's not as if Docherty was a great judge of a player. I acknowledge that he did a good job in his short spell as Scotland manager in 1971. But in club football he was sacked on numerous occasions by chairmen in England and abroad, with some of his spells in charge distinctly on the short side: at Queen's Park Rangers for example he lasted just twenty-nine days before being shown the door. That erratic record prompted his most famous quip: 'I had more clubs than Jack Nicklaus'. At Manchester United he achieved something that many thought impossible when he contrived to get the Old Trafford club relegated. Their demotion was confirmed on the penultimate day of the season in a derby with Man City when Denis Law, given a free transfer by Docherty just a year before, scored the goal that sent the Reds down.

Sir Alex Ferguson he ain't.

As for Buchan I have to be honest. I never liked the guy. I will never forget the time he walked up to me in a Scotland training camp and informed me that he was the better player. He may well have thought that but it is not the way you speak to your teammates. To my mind it is pure arrogance. I would never have dreamt of doing that to a colleague.

I was anxious all week until the team was announced, especially when I read every day in the papers that Buchan was the favourite to start. But when the news came I had good reason to celebrate. Willie Ormond had stuck by me, giving me my customary berth alongside Colin Jackson in the centre of defence. It would be my first ever game against England. A treble with Rangers and now I would be turning out in the oldest international fixture of them all; it really doesn't get any better than that. The atmosphere was, as you can imagine, sensational.

If the days of the 120,000-plus crowds at the old stadium had gone forever the noise created by the 85,167 souls who rolled up on 15 May 1976 was nothing to be sneezed at. It was the biggest game I had ever played in.

The teams:

Scotland: Rough, McGrain, Forsyth, Jackson, Donachie, Rioch, Masson, Gemmill, Dalglish, Jordan, Gray

England: Clemence, Todd, Thompson, McFarland, Mills, Keegan, Francis, Kennedy, Channon, Pearson, Taylor

The England eleven as you would expect was very strong, with guys like Ray Clemence, Colin Todd, Kevin Keegan and Mick Channon. Many of them had played at Wembley the year before and they clearly fancied their chances of turning us over again.

Let battle commence.

England were no doubt anticipating a tough fight but in the early stages they must have been revising that opinion. Quite simply we were too casual, too careless and too cocky. After our displays against Wales and Northern Ireland perhaps we thought we just had to turn up to win. It didn't take our opponents long to disabuse us of that notion. After eleven minutes England seized their opportunity. The ball was channelled out wide to Roy McFarland, who saw a gap in our defence and whipped in a great cross to the far post. He found an unmarked Channon, who bulleted a header past Roughie.

You could have heard a pin drop in the old stadium. I don't think our fans could believe the evidence of their own eyes. I have never felt so deflated on a football pitch.

It was then we showed what we were made of. There were some great footballers in our side but more than anything they had character. After the loss of the goal we were transformed. From that moment on we were magnificent. Don Masson got the equaliser in the eighteenth minute and then Kenny Dalglish got the winner four minutes after half time. It is one every Scot will remember: the one where Kenny put the ball through the legs of his future Liverpool teammate, Ray Clemence. I have to mention big Joe Jordan here. Sometimes he got a bit of stick for his goalscoring ratio but in this game he was superb and very unlucky not to score. It was fitting that the winner came from his marauding run down the left channel and pinpoint cross to Dalglish in the box.

For my own part I have never been so focused on a football pitch in my life. I went into every tackle as if my life depended on it and I am sure Keegan and Channon must have wondered what I was on. It was sheer adrenalin. Although I always gave 100 per cent, Docherty's remarks had fired me up to a degree I had never experienced before. Failure was simply not an option and I gave what was probably the performance of my life.

It could all have gone horribly wrong with just three minutes left on the clock. Mick Channon had burst through the middle of our defence and looked odds-on to score. I was the nearest Scotland player to him but I was too far away to catch him.

At least it would have been too far in any other game.

Somehow I managed to make up the space between me and the big Englishman. I got a challenge in and pushed the ball away from the danger area. Danger over. I suppose I have Docherty to thank for that tackle. To this day I still believe that I would never have made it but for the extra motivation his idiotic remark gave me.

We ran out victors by two goals to one, winning the home internationals outright for the first time since 1967. It was also the first time we had beaten the other three home countries since 1962. And how we celebrated, with wee Archie Gemmill leading us round the Hampden pitch in an impromptu lap of honour. Many of the England players didn't take it at all well. Channon couldn't wait to get off the pitch at time up, telling reporters that 'I couldn't stomach seeing those bastards run around in triumph.'

So no hard feelings then Mick?

The entire Scotland camp was elated by the victory, including the SFA blazers. I remember that after the win over Northern Ireland I had put my shorts, jersey and socks in my sports bag, thinking that it would be nice to have them as a souvenir. But when I came out of the shower, to my surprise, they had been removed from the bag by an SFA official, no doubt acting on orders from the powers-that-be. I couldn't believe it; to me that was such a petty way to behave.

But what a difference after we beat the English.

The guy who had taken the kit out of my bag after the Northern Ireland game had completely changed his tune. 'You can take them all,' he said, pointing to the Scotland strips.

Regarding the result and performance I was more than satisfied. I felt that I had done enough to cement my place in the side. Willie Ormond clearly agreed. He named Danny McGrain and me as Scotland's best players in the championships. The journalistic profession was also highly praiseworthy about my performance and didn't miss the opportunity to have a dig at Docherty. Two Sunday papers, the *Sunday Post* and the *Sunday Mail*, gave me five stars out of five with the *Mail* commenting that 'Tom Forsyth had a magnificent second half and totally justified his selection despite the claims of Old Trafford manager Tommy Docherty for Martin Buchan.' Doug Baillie in the *Post* was equally effusive, pointing out that I didn't allow Keegan or Channon a sniff of the ball. Hugh Taylor in the *Daily Record* took a similar line: 'Who said Forsyth can't play? There's class as well as power in Big Tam's play.' Taylor was also kind enough to describe my performance – and that of Danny McGrain – as 'world class'.

What about the bold Doc? After the game he claimed that his remarks had been exaggerated by the media and then he went on to praise my performance in glowing terms.

> It was a great result for Scotland. I was delighted for them. I was proved wrong on the day by Tom Forsyth and good luck to the lad. I can't praise him highly enough. He did everything asked of him and then added one or two extras.

I am glad he admitted he was wrong but he should never have said what he did. To me it is unforgivable for anyone in football – particularly a man who had managed the national team – to use such derogatory terms about a fellow professional.

On a lighter note my grandfather had actually bred Clydesdale horses and they are magnificent animals, thoroughbreds in their own right.

13

Scotland's Greatest Year

If season 1976/77 was my most disappointing to date as a Ranger it was exactly the opposite at international level. It really was our annus mirabilis. We not only won the home internationals for the second year in a row – including a famous win at Wembley – but we also laid the foundations for World Cup qualification in 1978. If that wasn't enough there was also a highly creditable close-season tour to South America in which we had the honour of turning out against Brazil in the Maracana stadium. I am delighted to say I was right at the heart of all three events.

Despite the glories to come that particular phase of my international career didn't actually start that well. I did play in a friendly against Finland on 8 September 1976, which we won 6–0. It was so easy that some papers described it as 'shooting practice', while the manager of Czechoslovakia, who we would face in the World Cup qualifiers, said that Scotland was the best team in Europe. That was high praise indeed considering his team had won the European Championships just a few months before.

Then just when things were going so well I got injured playing for my club, causing me to miss a whole chunk of Rangers games in the autumn and early winter. It also meant of course that I had to sit out the two World Cup qualifiers against Czechoslovakia away and against

Wales at Hampden.[21] My old rival Martin Buchan was drafted in to play alongside big Gordon McQueen and my fear was that Willie Ormond would keep faith with that combination.

I was delighted therefore to be picked for the next squad, a friendly against Sweden at Hampden in April 1977. There were many call-offs – you always expect them before friendlies – and whether it was because of a lack of alternatives or the fact that Ormond considered me first choice I was reinstated to the side. It was a good one to play in, not just because Scotland won 3–1 but also because we played really well. I was the man in possession and the manager must have been satisfied with an excellent all-round performance.

Then, as so often happens in football, everything changed in an instant. Willie Ormond, unhappy with his contract, left the Scotland hot-seat to take over at Hearts. I felt it was a blow for the national side. His record was excellent, taking us to the World Cup finals for the first time in sixteen years in 1974 and of course lifting the home-international championships in 1976.[22] He was a quiet guy, not a bawler or a shouter, nor what you would call a great tactician, but he had the knack of picking the right players and getting the best out of them. His playing record undoubtedly helped him in the eyes of the dressing room. He had been a member of the legendary Hibs forward line – the so-called Famous Five of Smith, Johnstone, Reilly, Turnbull and Ormond – that helped the Easter Road club win three league championships in the late 1940s and early 1950s.

Players are always apprehensive about a new manager coming in. He has a blank canvas, the opportunity to start again with his own

---

[21] We lost by two goals to nil in Prague, a game in which Andy Gray was ordered off after a punch-up with Ondrus, the Czech skipper, who was also sent for an early bath. However, we managed to beat Wales 1–0 at Hampden.

[22] It should also be remembered that in the 1970s only sixteen teams qualified for World Cup finals, not thirty-two like today, making it twice as hard to qualify. That makes Scotland's achievement of remaining unbeaten in the tournament all the more creditable, even if we did not advance to the second phase.

men. The question is: will you be one of them? The hot favourite for
the job was Jock Stein, which at the time I thought would be good for
the national team and for me. After all he was a great manager and on
a personal level it was strongly rumoured that he had been interested
in signing me when I was still playing Junior football. But as so often
happens in football there was a fly in the ointment. Jock had just won
the league-and-cup double and was generally considered to be back to
his best after his car accident. He now fancied Celtic's chances in the
European Cup and so he informed the SFA that he would only take the
Scotland job on a part-time basis. That was ruled out by the powers-
that-be in Park Gardens, who went to the next name on their short list.

One Alistair Reid MacLeod.

I was of course well aware of Ally. I had often faced his Ayr United
team both at Motherwell and Rangers. You always got a hard game
against them, especially at Somerset Park. With fifteen to twenty
thousand packed inside that little stadium and Ally going berserk on
the touchline the Ayr boys were, without fail, up for it. And they could
play a bit too. I think I am right in saying that Ally built the strongest
team in their history, one that regularly gave the Old Firm and other
much bigger clubs a going over on their own midden. He was just as
successful at Aberdeen, winning the League Cup in 1976 and taking
the Dons to second place in the championship. With a record like that
it is no wonder the SFA were on his trail.

Ally was appointed Scotland manager in May 1977, just in time
for the home internationals. The question was: how did he rate Tom
Forsyth? I didn't have to wait long to find out. I was named in the
squad and it was then that I really got to know the remarkable man
who had just become our manager.

The first thing you noticed about Ally was his passion for football.
It was a genuine love affair; that is the only way I can describe it. He
talked about the game non-stop; I am sure he even dreamt about it.
The second thing I noticed was the man's self-confidence. When he
got the squad together his opening line told you everything you needed
to know.

'My name is Ally MacLeod and I am a winner.'

I was impressed. We all were. His sheer enthusiasm, if perhaps a little un-Scottish, was infectious. With such a positive, ebullient guy in charge who knew what heights we could hit.

Our first game was away to Wales, who at that time played some of their their home games at the Racecourse Ground, Wrexham FC's modest little stadium. I don't know if I would have been first pick or not but Buchan was injured and I started alongside Gordon McQueen. Wales were a very strong team in those days, with guys like Leighton James, Terry Yorath and John Toshack in their ranks. In fact they had just beaten Czechoslovakia in a European Championship qualifier and would go on to beat England in the home internationals that year. The game itself was goalless and entirely forgettable but I was the man in possession and determined to stay there.

Next up was Northern Ireland at Hampden and for the second year in a row we beat them by three goals to nil. If truth be told it was even easier than 1976 and I certainly don't recall having to do much defending. Now for England.

I know there is a lot of hype surrounding the World Cup and the European Championship and I fully accept that the football is of a higher order. But at that time playing against the Auld Enemy at Wembley was for most Scotsmen a career pinnacle. I had been on the bench for the corresponding fixture in 1973, when we lost 1–0, and while that had been a great experience I was desperate to get on the pitch. The Tartan Army felt the same way about the fixture and the aura that surrounded it, and such was their fervour that many of them financed their biennial trips to London by putting a couple of quid away each week into 'Wembley clubs'. Quite simply it was the game that transfixed a nation.

The scenes on Wembley Way that hot June afternoon as our coach struggled through the tens of thousands of Scotland fans had to be seen to be believed. I have never experienced anything like it, not even at Hampden. These people wanted us to win so much it hurt. There was no way we could let them down.

If the coach trip was emotionally draining that was as nothing compared to the atmosphere inside the stadium. As I walked down the tunnel and onto that hallowed turf I discovered that one hoary old cliché is literally true: the hairs on your neck really do stand up at moments like that. To be met by forty-plus thousand tartan-bedecked

Scotsmen singing their hearts out was truly inspiring; perhaps even a little frightening in its intensity. I was also chuffed that the fans had composed a little ditty about me, one that harked back to our meeting with England the year before:

They call him Jaws
He's got Channon by the baws
Tom Forsyth, Tom Forsyth

For a moment my thoughts drifted back, back to Stonehouse where I knew my family, friends and neighbours would all be watching . . . and hoping. I prayed that I wouldn't let them down.

The teams:

Scotland: Rough, McGrain, Forsyth, McQueen, Donachie, Rioch, Masson, Hartford, Dalglish, Jordan, Johnston
England: Clemence, Neal, Watson, Hughes, Mills, Greenhoff, Talbot, Kennedy, Francis, Channon, Pearson

Looking at the two sides I honestly believe that we were, on paper, stronger than them and it isn't often you can say that about a Scotland–England game. We had quality players in every department, many more than the opposition. Now we had to prove it.

In fact we were quite brilliant that day. Big Gordon McQueen got our first goal with a towering header from a corner and Dalglish added a second. They got a penalty with three minutes to go, which Channon converted, but it was really only a consolation. The 2–1 score-line flattered them because we were on top for almost the whole ninety minutes. The bottom line was that as well as beating the English we had retained the home-international championships.

As you can imagine the Scottish press had a field day, with some getting carried away by the result and the performance. In the *Daily Record* a veteran sportswriter who you think might have known better seemed to lose the plot completely, arguing that the class of 77 'might turn into the greatest who ever wore the blue of the country' and for good measure he hailed the manager 'as a great football brain,' something that Ally, despite his supreme self-confidence, would never have claimed for himself. But that is the Scottish media for you. Given the slightest encouragement they will write up the national team as the greatest thing since sliced bread.

It's not just the media. I think that all Scots get carried away when it comes to football and if that victory was greeted ecstatically by the press it was mirrored by the reaction of the fans. At full time they poured onto the lush turf of Wembley in their tens of thousands. You will remember those unforgettable scenes as the Tartan Army dug up the pitch, tore down the crossbars and flattened the goalposts as they hunted for a souvenir. If proof was need about how we Scots feel about beating England at anything, but especially football, it was provided that sunny afternoon in north London.

Dozens of our fans ended up in court on the Monday morning charged with criminal damage, breach of the peace and assorted misdemeanours. I don't think there was any real malice involved, despite what many of the English pundits said. To me if the fans were guilty of anything it was of letting off steam. We are a football-crazy country and we had just beaten our fiercest rivals – rather easily as it happens – in their own backyard. What did the authorities expect?

The exploits of our fans have passed into legend and one in particular made me laugh. A guy from Maybole admitted to the magistrates that he had cut up the Wembley turf but in his defence he explained that the sod came from the exact spot that Kenny Dalglish had scored from! His intention was to take the turf home, put it a jar on his mantelpiece and watch it grow. That, he said, would help him 'to remember the match'. His explanation didn't cut much ice with the beak. He was fined £50 and in addition was ordered to pay £50 compensation to the FA.

My only gripe was that I didn't get a medal from the SFA for winning the home internationals either in 1976 or in 1977. That annoyed me. I have heard that medals were struck and that some guys got them. If that is true – and I cannot say for sure that it is – I certainly didn't get one. It would have been a nice memento of what after all was a notable achievement. Some people might think that is sour grapes, reasoning that as I played for Scotland twenty-two times I must have a whole bunch of caps in a display cabinet at home to commemorate my international career. But that is not the case. I have only three 'physical' caps, simply because in those days they were awarded on a season-by-season basis, or so I am led to believe. I am not sure if more caps were sent out by the SFA, perhaps to Ibrox, and were not passed on to me. Maybe one day I will find out.

* * *

As it happens I didn't get much time to savour our achievements. Because just a matter of days later I was on a plane bound for Chile, where we would play the first match of our summer tour of South America. It was a gruelling end to a long season that had included – for most Scotland players – domestic and European competitions with their clubs as well as World Cup qualifiers, international friendlies and the home internationals. You can bet your bottom dollar it wouldn't happen now but the guys who played in my era were less cosseted than the players of today. The SFA's logic I think was that the World Cup finals were due to be played in Argentina the following year and given that we had a good chance of qualifying we needed to acclimatise ourselves.

It was particularly hard on guys like me who had young children. We would be away from our wives and families for most of June and there was absolutely no chance of us getting to see them when we were in South America. Nowadays wives and girlfriends are flown out to the countries in which tournaments are taking place but that would have been unthinkable in those far-off days. We hear so much today about the WAG phenomenon but in the 1970s a wag was a guy who told funny stories!

To be quite honest I was keen to be on the tour, despite the fact that I was still bothered by a pain in my groin, an injury that had I had been carrying for the whole season. I was desperate to play in the World Cup finals and at age twenty-eight I reasoned this might be my last chance. If I did right by Ally he would, I hoped, do right by me.

I might not have been so keen if I had realised just what was happening politically in Latin America at the time. Revolution was in the air in two of the countries we were to visit – Chile and Argentina – and that made it a surreal and at times quite frightening experience. The first game was against Chile. The country was still going through huge turmoil following a military coup in 1973, in which General

Augusto Pinochet had replaced communist Salvador Allende as president. The capital, Santiago, was known as the 'city of fear' and when we arrived there curfews were still being imposed during the hours of darkness. It was even said that protestors had been tortured and shot in the very stadium in which we were to take on the host nation.

Despite that we got our heads down and prepared for the game against Chile. In terms of performance we continued where we had left off against England, running out comfortable winners by four goals to two, with wee Lou Macari helping himself to a double. By any standards it was an excellent result and it showed just how strong we were in those days. I felt I played well in unfamiliar surroundings alongside Martin Buchan in the centre of defence.

Our next opponents were Argentina, and to say that our sojourn there was memorable would be the understatement of the century. In fact getting into the capital, Buenos Aires, without being shot was an achievement in itself. Like Chile the Argentine political system was going through a very turbulent and violent period and was under the control of the regime that would invade the Falkland Islands in 1982. The opposition was intent on having the forthcoming World Cup moved away from Argentina and one way of doing that was by disrupting sporting events, for example Scotland's game in the Boca stadium. There was little sign of trouble at the airport and the coach journey from there to our hotel – which the England team, also on tour that year, had just vacated – was uneventful.

Uneventful that is until we reached downtown Buenos Aires.

We were happily bowling along the capital's most fashionable shopping street taking in the sights when, without warning, the bus sharply accelerated. A voice shouted at us to get down on the floor and as we sped off at sixty miles per hour we heard the unmistakeable wail of police sirens. After what we had witnessed in Chile we knew this was no exercise and that something must have happened to give the police cause for concern. The next thing we knew we had arrived at the hotel, where we were told that word had reached the authorities of a possible kidnap attempt. Security was very tight for the rest of the stay in Buenos Aires, with armed guards positioned outside our hotel rooms.

If security was an issue off the pitch we soon discovered that things were not any better on it. There is only one word I can use to describe a section of the Argentine team: animals. They kicked, punched, gouged and spat their way through the ninety minutes. That surprised me.[23] They had great players in their team, skilful players, players who didn't resort either to violence or to cheating, players like Daniel Passarella, Osvaldo Ardiles and Mario Kempes. A lot of the others were also technically proficient but for some reason they were more interested in the darker football arts.

Although we all suffered that night Willie Johnston was singled out for special attention. Right from the word go he was kicked and hacked mercilessly and for someone not known for an even temperament he did well to retaliate only once, for which of course he was booked. But everyone has their breaking point and when Pernia fouled him for, oh, the ninety-ninth time Bud said something to him and the Argentine spat right in his face. Then, just a few minutes later, the most incredible thing happened. Pernia punched Willie in the kidneys and was rightly ordered off. But Mr Arppi, the Brazilian referee, also decided to send Willie off despite the fact that he had taken the most horrific abuse. To me it was a cowardly decision by the referee, who I thought was intimidated right from the first minute by the partisan home crowd.

I had a taste of their cynicism myself when one of their substitutes, Trossero, brushed past me in the penalty box and then threw himself spectacularly to the floor. The guy would have won the Olympic diving gold. So you can imagine our dismay when the referee awarded them a penalty, which for some teams might have been the final straw. But, if anything, it made us even more determined to get a result. Our mindset was that we weren't going to give in to these gangsters in football strips. (The *Daily Record* agreed, describing the Argentines as 'Mafia

---

[23] Argentina's reputation for on-field violence was well deserved. They tried to kick England off the park during the 1966 World Cup and their club teams weren't much better as both Celtic and Manchester United found to their cost when they faced Racing Club (1967) and Estudiantes (1968) respectively in the World Club championships.

Hit Men' and praising the Scotland team for not retaliating despite the astonishing levels of intimidation.) Looking back I am really glad that despite everything they threw at us we escaped with a 1–1 draw.

We were all understandably delighted to leave Argentina. It wasn't just because of the way we had been treated there. We were excited by the prospect of facing our third and last opponents on the tour: Brazil. It is a dream come true for any professional player to test himself against the best and Brazil then, as now, were right at the top of the tree. They might have had a mediocre World Cup in 1974 by their own lofty standards (being eliminated in the semi-final by Holland) but they could still field a team of superstars, guys like Zico, Rivellino, Paulo Cesar, Gil, Ze Maria and the great goalkeeper, Leao. This time we would be playing a team whose aim would be to play, rather than kick, us off the park.

Scotland: Rough, McGrain, Donachie, Buchan, Forsyth, Rioch, Masson, Dalglish, Gemmill, Hartford, Johnston

And play us off the park they did. We defended well – in truth we had little option – but could not get in a meaningful blow in attack. In fact we didn't even get a single corner, such was Brazil's dominance. I could make excuses – we were missing important players like Jordan, Gray and Macari through injury and the game was after all being played at the end of an exceptionally long and arduous season – but the fact was that they were simply outstanding. You had to hand it to them; these guys passed and moved better than any opposition team I had ever come up against. If their young striker, Zico, was the new superstar in the making then Roberto Rivellino in midfield was the beating heart of the team, an experienced campaigner with every trick in the book and then some.[24] He strolled effortlessly through the

---

[24] Zico, often known as the 'White Pele', was probably the greatest player in the world during the late 1970s and early 1980s. He is by general consent the best player never to have won a World Cup medal. Rivellino is ranked among the top five Brazilian players of all time, alongside Pele, Garrincha, Ronaldo and his teammate that night, Zico. He was a member of the Brazil team that lifted the World Cup in 1970 (rated by many observers as the greatest of all time) and he won more than one hundred caps for his country.

game, pinging forty-yard passes to the feet of his teammates. At times we just couldn't get close to them and Roughie, inevitably, had a busy night in goal. In fact he kept us in the game with a string of great saves.

As is often the way we found that you can't defend for a whole game and not concede. We held out until the seventieth minute, when the inevitable happened. They were awarded a free kick twenty-five yards from our goal. Up stepped Zico, who blasted the ball into the top-right-hand corner of our net. Alan had no chance; such was the pace and swerve Zico got on the ball that it would have left any goalkeeper in the world floundering. Four minutes later it really was all over when they got a second, Rivellino-inspired, goal.

I was disappointed at the final whistle, but not downhearted. After all how many Scots have played in the world-famous Maracana stadium in front of 100,000 fans? That, for a young lad from a mining village in Lanarkshire, was an incredible thrill, a memory that will live with me forever. I didn't let myself down either. With the decisive World Cup qualifiers to come in the autumn of 1977 I hoped that I had done enough to retain my place in the squad.

* * *

The second and final part of the drama that was the qualifying campaign for the 1978 World Cup would be played out in September and October 1977. It couldn't have been tighter. We had two points from two games, as did the other two countries in our three-team group, Czechoslovakia and Wales. The first hurdle was Czechoslovakia, who had won the European Championships in 1976, defeating West Germany in the final.[25] The Czechs had already beaten us, by two goals to nil, in the first qualifying game in Prague. Putting one over on a team like that, even at Hampden, would be a formidable task for anyone.

---

[25] West Germany were, of course, reigning world champions when they met Czechoslovakia in the 1976 final. The Germans had luminaries like Franz Beckenbauer, Sepp Maier, Berti Vogts and Uli Hoeness in their side.

However, in the run up to the game, it became clear that not every-thing in the Czech garden was rosy. Their outstanding keeper, Ivo Viktor, had retired while three of their other leading players – man-mountain centre half and captain Ondrus (suspended), attacking midfielder Panenka (injured) and striker Petras (off form) – would also be missing at Hampden. All four had played leading roles in the Czechs' recent successes and they were top international players by any standards.

In addition Czechoslovakia were now under new management. Coach Vaclav Jazek, who had guided them to their Euro triumph, was ill. So a new man was at the helm. His name? Dr Josef Venglos. Yes: the same Dr Jo who was such a dismal failure as manager of Celtic in the 1998/99 season, when his team was second-best to a treble-winning Rangers side managed by Dick Advocaat.

The upshot of all this upheaval was that Czechoslovakia's form had slumped alarmingly. When they beat us in Prague in October 1976 they had been on a run of twenty-four games undefeated but after that game their record for the next seven fixtures was much less impressive: won two, lost four and drawn one. Those defeats included a 3–0 reverse in Wrexham against group rivals Wales. We knew we had a real chance: the Czechs were still top class but they were no longer the all-conquering heroes of old.

Events just seemed to conspire against poor old Dr Jo and his players. Coming over for the Wednesday evening qualifier at Hampden their flight from Prague was delayed, which meant that they missed their connection at Heathrow. The only option available was to travel overnight on the sleeper train, which meant they got into Glasgow at seven o'clock on the Tuesday morning. Citing fatigue the Czechs asked for the game to be postponed for twenty-four hours until the Thursday night, a request that was promptly rejected by FIFA.

To be honest the Czechs' misfortunes made no difference to Ally MacLeod. He would have been just as confident even if Pele, Cruyff and Beckenbauer had been playing for the opposition. In the days before the game he was as bullish as ever, telling the papers 'We will win. There's no doubt about it.'

I think the players felt the same way. After winning the home internationals and doing so well in South America we feared no one, especially at home.

Scotland: Rough, Jardine, McQueen, Forsyth, McGrain, Masson, Rioch, Hartford, Dalglish, Jordan, Johnston

That was our eleven but I will never forget our twelfth man that night. The Scotland fans. The day after the game I wrote a column for the *Evening Times* and I went out of my way to praise the backing they gave us. It was quite incredible and as I ran out of the Hampden tunnel and heard them singing their hearts out I thought to myself:

'I'm Scottish, I'm wearing the Scottish blue and I'll give everything I have for the fans.'

I just couldn't let those people down.

In a nutshell we brushed the European champions aside, playing with power, purpose and not a little skill. I would have to rank it as the best performance by any Scotland team that I played in. Roared on by 85,000 of our fans we were simply irresistible. Big Joe Jordan got the first after eighteen minutes, Asa Hartford added the second nine minutes before half-time and Kenny Dalglish rounded it off with the third ten minutes into the second period. They got a consolation ten minutes from the end, making the final score 3–1.

We hadn't just beaten a world-class team. We had completely out-played them, so much so that Dr Jo and his coaching team felt the need to bring up that hoary old chestnut: that we had used roughhouse British tactics and kicked them off the park. I felt, along with the rest of the team, that what he said was sour grapes. I have always believed that the best place to do your talking is on the park – then you won't need to whinge about the opposition or the referee after the game.

The equation was now quite simple: beat Wales on 12 October 1977 and we were on the plane to Argentina. In fact under certain circumstances even a draw might have been enough, not that Ally was contemplating such an eventuality. After defeating the European champions so comprehensively I think that he, in common with the whole Scottish nation, believed that it would be something of a formality. The facts seemed to support that view. Wales had not beaten Scotland since 1964 and in ninety-one games between the teams Scotland had won fifty-five, Wales just fifteen with twenty-one drawn.

The bookies agreed, making us 4/5 favourites with Wales at 7/2 against, despite the fact that it was their home fixture. The papers too gave Wales little chance, seeing the game as little more than a formality and noting that many of their players plied their trade with unfashionable, lower-division clubs like Burnley, Wrexham and Hull.

We Scots however do have a tendency to get carried away, especially in matters football-related. Wales had a strong and capable side at that time, one that included John Toshack, Terry Yorath, Joey Jones and Mickey Thomas, although fortunately for us their most dangerous player, winger Leighton James of Derby County, was injured and would not play. So we would have to be at our very best against a side that was desperate to qualify for its first finals since 1958. Not that our manager was at all bothered who would, or wouldn't play, for Wales. A few days before the game he made a quite startling statement to reporters: 'To hell with Wales. I don't give a damn who plays for them. The team I put out will be too good for them.' So none of that measured, circumspect, always-respect-your-opponents nonsense from Ally!

The anticipation in Scotland was massive, with tens of thousands of Scottish fans poised to make the short journey to Wales for the final and deciding game. In fact it was the sheer number of people expected to travel that led to a decision being taken to move the match to Anfield, home of Liverpool FC. Wales in those days did not have a national football stadium and played home matches at either the home of Cardiff City, Ninian Park, or at the little Racecourse Ground, which was owned by Wrexham. Neither was anywhere near big enough for an international match of this importance between two British sides.

Once that decision was made the game effectively became a home game for us. Unlike in Scotland football at that time was not the number-one sport in Wales and it may still, even today, be in second place behind rugby. So the number of Wales fans who would travel to Liverpool was always going to be a fraction of those coming down from north of the border. If I had been in the shoes of the Welsh FA there is no way I would have moved what was one of the biggest games in their history, no matter how much money was at stake. But they did and I felt that gave us a huge advantage.

With up to eighty thousand Scots on the march the city of Liverpool battened down the hatches. All police leave was cancelled and a ring of steel was thrown around Anfield by the five hundred officers on duty, many with guard dogs. The stadium had a seventeen-foot wall round the perimeter, built after Celtic fans had scaled the old wall before a European tie in 1966. Inside the ground eight-foot high fences, tipped with broken glass or spikes, were erected to discourage pitch invasions.[26]

Every Scot will remember the atmosphere that game generated, whether they were inside Anfield or watched it on the telly. It can't be put into words; it was that special. If there were any Welsh fans there for their 'home' game nobody either saw or heard them. I think it showed to the world what we Scots have known all along: that Scotland is the most football-mad country on earth, more so even than Brazil.

Having been a first pick for some time I was reasonably confident that I would be in the side. But my cause wasn't helped by an ankle knock I had taken against Dundee United on the Saturday before Anfield. To miss one of the nation's biggest games for years would have been sickening, but I got treatment from the Scotland medic, Dr Fitzsimmons – who as it happened was also the Celtic doctor – and in the nick of time I was declared fit. This meant that the manager was able to slot me into my usual berth in central defence alongside big Gordon McQueen.

Scotland: Rough, Jardine, Forsyth, McQueen, Donachie, Masson, Macari, Hartford, Johnston, Dalglish, Jordan

When the game got under way we were like men possessed, putting Wales under severe pressure right from kick-off. Chances were made and chances were spurned and I remember thinking after fifteen minutes that we should have been three up. I prayed that the misses wouldn't come back to haunt us.

The tide began to turn. For some reason – perhaps it was the sheer weight of expectation – we became edgy. Passes went astray, fifty-fifty

---

[26] In fact the Scottish fans conducted themselves very well, and the only arrests were for drunkenness. Their behaviour was later praised by the Liverpool police.

tackles were lost, crosses failed to beat the first defender. They had a tidy midfield of Yorath, Mahoney and Flynn and began to take a grip on the game. It was frustrating. We knew we were a cut above them but nerves seemed to have got the better of us and no matter how much we huffed and puffed it was to no avail. Wales piled on the pressure and Alan Rough came to our rescue on several occasions, the most memorable being an acrobatic save from a John Toshack lob. How Roughie managed to tip it onto the bar I will never know.

Then, after seventy-eight minutes, we got out of jail with the most controversial goal in Scotland's history.

Bud Johnston threw in a diagonal cross from the left and Joe Jordan, who was surrounded by a phalanx of red jerseys, jumped. It was clear to the world and his wife that someone in that ruck of players had played the ball, but not with his head. It was the clearest handball you will ever see. Our forwards and the 50,000 Scots inside Anfield immediately roared 'penalty'. And the French referee – Monsieur Robert Wurtz – no doubt influenced by the passion of the crowd, gave it. The Wales players were raging, as was their manager, Mike Smith, but it cut no ice with the ref. Robert Wurtz had made his decision and that was that.

We know now of course that it was Joe Jordan who handled the ball, but there was no way he could admit it, at least not while the game was in progress. The nation's hopes were on his shoulders. I have never met the player who would make an admission like that during such a vital match, no matter what the pundits and barrack-room lawyers might argue. It was similar to the Thierry Henry incident in the World Cup playoff game against the Republic of Ireland in November 2009, when the France striker clearly controlled the ball with his hand before crossing it for Gallas to score. Henry accepted the goal, but then we all would in his shoes.

In the interests of full disclosure I must record that I too have conned a referee. It wasn't in a World Cup match but in the distinctly unglamorous surroundings of Somerset Park. I was playing in midfield for Motherwell in a league match against Ayr United when I burst into the box while chasing a fifty-fifty ball. Out of the corner of my eye I could see that the referee was behind a ruck of players and probably unsighted. When the Ayr defender and I came together I saw my chance and went down, even though the guy had hardly touched me. Penalty!

Did I feel guilty? Not in the slightest. I didn't expect the referee to give a penalty but I was happy to take it because forwards often did it to me.

Joe Harper was in my view quite the master when it came to getting dodgy penalties. I remember one game at Ibrox when the wee man played for Hibs. We were defending the Celtic end and a ball was knocked into the box. Joe went to collect the ball, with me in close pursuit. He knew I was on his tail so he immediately took a dive, one that would have been given 9.9 for technical merit by an Olympic judge. I never touched him but Hibs were awarded the penalty, which they duly converted. I was sore about that one but I knew it was part and parcel of the professional game. It doesn't stop me giving Joe stick whenever I see him. My usual greeting when we meet up is: 'You wee bastard. I still remember you diving that day in the box and I fell for it.' But it is on professional, and not moral, grounds that I am berating him – it is because he outwitted me and gained an advantage for his team. It was my professional pride that was hurt.

I know that diving and other forms of gamesmanship are a red rag to a bull for fans and pundits but then they aren't the ones who have to make a living from what happens on the field. That's just the way it is and I am afraid it isn't going to change any time soon.

That little digression over we can return to Anfield.

In such a cauldron it took real nerve to step up and take that penalty but Don Masson showed a captain's courage by coolly sending the keeper the wrong way. We were on our way.

Kenny Dalglish's goal from sub Martin Buchan's cross was the icing on the cake. We had won by two goals to nil and were in the World Cup finals. As Arthur Montford – the legendary 'talking sports jacket' – said in his television commentary: 'Argentina here we come'.

The only slight dampener on Anfield was that the police wouldn't let us do a lap of honour, something that enraged Ally. That however was a mere detail. We were going to the World Cup finals, to the greatest show on earth and given our outstanding form over the past two years who was to say we wouldn't do well when we got there. We were the only British team to make it, England having been eliminated by Italy, which made our success all the sweeter.

When I look back at my international career from the perspective of 2010 I can't help but reflect on what a truly wonderful time it was. That eighteen-month period from the middle of 1976 to the end of 1977 must rank as one of the most productive in Scotland's history. We won back-to-back home-international championships, beating the Auld Enemy twice along the way. We qualified for the World Cup finals, knocking out the reigning European champions and a very dangerous Wales team. Most of all we had played some great football in what I would call the true Scottish tradition: with pace, power and determination. It was an honour to play alongside world-class players like Souness, Dalglish, Jordan, McGrain and Jardine. What a pity we don't have guys of that calibre today. I must also mention our fans; they gave us such tremendous backing, and conducted themselves well, broken crossbars at Wembley notwithstanding!

It was a privilege to be part of it.

14

A Second Treble and the Coming of Coop

After winning back the league from Celtic in 1975 and then lifting the treble in 1976 we had every reason to look forward to an excellent season in 1976/77. But as Rabbie Burns sagely observes, 'The best laid plans gang aft aglay.' We should have built on what had gone before but for a whole range of reasons we went backwards. Injuries played a big part. I lost most of October and November to a knee injury and other regular first-teamers like Derek Johnstone, Colin Jackson and John Greig missed many important games too.

It was the first half of the season that did for us. We won only two of our opening eight league games, very poor by Rangers standards. It wasn't just the bigger teams we had trouble with; I remember we lost to both Partick Thistle and Motherwell within the space of seven days (although I didn't play in either game). Despite good runs in the winter and spring we were always playing catch up with Celtic, who eventually won the league by taking nine more points than us, a huge gap considering it was two points for a win in those days.

Nor was it much better in the cup competitions. We did get to the League Cup semi-final but were trounced 5–1 by Aberdeen, another game that I missed. In the Scottish Cup we made the final but lost a scrappy, physical, bad-tempered match to Celtic, who won 1–0 thanks to a disputed penalty awarded by R. B. 'Bob' Valentine and converted by Andy Lynch.

At least we had the European Cup, a competition that many observers had tipped us to win after the glories of our treble season. But that too went belly up. When we were drawn to meet FC Zurich of Switzerland in the first round the form book suggested we were onto a good thing. Switzerland is hardly a hotbed of football and the men from Zurich were part-time players. It was also just a few short years since we had lifted a European trophy and many of the heroes of Barcelona were still at the club. But it turned out to be one of our most dismal experiences on the European stage.

In the first leg at Ibrox we lost a sloppy goal in the opening minutes and then huffed and puffed our way through the rest of the game. We did manage to snatch an equaliser through Derek Parlane but a 1–1 score line at home is rarely a good result. And so it proved as we crashed out of the competition after losing by a single goal in Zurich.[27]

The other problem that season was the size of the crowds, especially at Ibrox. Our average dropped from about 30,000 in 75/76 to around 23,000 in 76/77. Clearly, the fans were not happy with the product on offer and were voting with their feet. I don't think it was just about results. Many fans, and the media, felt that we were a hard, tough-tackling, never-say-die outfit that in the absence of any discernible flair had no option but to grind out results. Jock Wallace, to a certain extent, agreed. What many people don't realise is that beneath his tough, no-nonsense persona there lurked a football purist. He was in fact a lover of good football, not for its own sake but because he believed it was the most effective way of winning games. However, to do that he recognised that Rangers would need a different type of player, a player that was comfortable on the ball, a player that could deliver a defence-splitting pass, a player that could turn a game with a swivel of the hips.

So in the summer of 1977 he went into the transfer market – and by god he delivered. Gordon Smith was signed from Kilmarnock for

[27] The only consolation, if you can call it that, was that Zurich reached the semi-finals, where they were eliminated by eventual winners, Liverpool.

a fee of £65,000. Gordon was a very pleasant guy, who quickly fitted into the dressing room, and he wasn't a bad player either. Skilful, quick and intelligent, he was known as Casper (after the cartoon character) because of his ability to ghost past players. Smith scored thirty-five goals for Rangers in about a hundred games, not bad for an attacking midfielder. Although I wasn't surprised when he became a radio and television pundit (not to mention a football agent) at the end of his career, I must admit I was a little surprised when he got the top job in Scottish football as chief executive of the SFA. You just don't expect former players to get jobs like that, although it made a pleasant change from the blazer brigade.

Big Jock's second capture was Bobby Russell, a nineteen-year-old midfielder, who came to Ibrox from Junior outfit Shettleston. A technically gifted midfielder, who excelled in the playmaker role, Russell made a fantastic contribution to Rangers during his ten years at the club, winning many honours along the way. Two very shrewd signings but the manager also brought in a guy who has become a legend down Govan way, and who to me is the most skilful player I have ever seen, bar none. His name was Davie Cooper.

What can you say about this guy that hasn't been said already? Moody? Undoubtedly. Unpredictable? Certainly. Hated training? Without question. But this guy, a steal from Clydebank at £100,000, was without doubt a footballer extraordinaire. I saw it every day at training. He neither liked running nor the two- or three-touch games that were a feature of our training sessions. The reason was simple. He just wanted to be on the ball all the time. And once he was on it he would screen and hug and cuddle it. You could never get the bloody thing off him. Then there were his little party pieces, like putting the ball through your legs. He nutmegged me every day on the training field. 'Bastard,' I would shout as he left me floundering in his wake, while aiming a kick at his backside!

People today rave about players like Messi, Ronaldo and Torres. And rightly so. They are fantastic players: technically brilliant, athletic and, most important of all, productive. But none of them were as skilful as Davie Cooper. What a talent he was. If I have a criticism of Coop it was his consistency, or lack of it. It really depended on which side of the bed he got out of. If he had focused as hard as some of the guys today, and had been positive in every game, he would have been one of the all-time greats of world football. No shadow of a doubt about that.

There are so many stories I could tell about Coop. But the one that still makes me laugh today concerns the goal he scored in the 1987/88 League Cup final at Hampden. Rangers were playing Aberdeen, who had Scotland goalkeeper Jim Leighton as the last line of defence. Rangers got a free kick just outside the box, very much in Coop territory. He ran up and fired an Exocet missile into the roof of the net. There was neither bend nor dip. It was pure power and accuracy. No keeper in history would have got anywhere near it, which is why I find Jim Leighton's statement after the game quite laughable. He and Coop were chatting about the goal, when Jim claimed.

'I got a touch to it.'

'Aye, on the way back out,' replied Davie, deadpan.

* * *

Those three signings in the summer of 1977 demonstrate that Big Jock liked to play football the right way. He had added flair by the bucket load and when you put them alongside the guys already at Ibrox – your Greigs, Jardines, Jacksons, MacDonalds and Johnstones – it added up to one powerful squad.

Jock Wallace was obviously pleased with my contribution, both in training and on the park, telling the *Sunday Mail* that 'Tom Forsyth is an example to every player here. He is now among the best central defenders in Europe at the age of twenty-eight. He has made progress every season and right now he is a legend in his own time.' You have no idea how a compliment like that from a guy of Jock's stature makes you feel. Forgive the cliché but I really did feel ten feet tall.

The early signs were good. We took on Southampton in a friendly at Ibrox and beat them 3–1 with, I thought, something to spare. Managed by Lawrie McMenemy the Saints were a top-tier outfit in those days and could parade a galaxy of stars, guys like Alan Ball and Peter Osgood. Then, as so often happens, football kicked us in the teeth.

Our first league game was away to Billy McNeill's Aberdeen. Due to injury we went into that fixture with a young side that included 16-year-old Billy McKay, Bobby McKean and Bobby Russell. The Dons – with luminaries like Bobby Clark, Willie Miller, Drew Jarvie and Joe Harper – were just too good on the day and won comfortably by three goals to one. Our first home fixture was if anything even worse. We slumped to a 2–0 defeat to Hibs, which meant we were rock bottom of the league after two games.

It was then that I discovered just how fickle some fans – and the media – can be.

As we walked off the pitch at the end of the Hibs game the boos rang out, a not untypical scenario when Rangers lose at home. But this time it was different. Some of the fans were calling for the head of Jock Wallace: the man who had been instrumental in bringing the European Cup Winners Cup to Ibrox; the man who had stopped Celtic from making it ten in a row; the man who had guided us to a treble just fifteen short months before. I couldn't believe it. Jock lived and breathed Rangers. No one could have worked harder or been more passionate in the club's cause. Yet here were so-called Rangers fans doing their utmost to get the man the sack. Whether or not they were frustrated by our failure to win a trophy during the previous season was to me irrelevant – he needed and deserved the support of every bluenose to get through a difficult period.

Sections of the media were even worse. The paper with the biggest sales in the country, the *Sunday Mail*, actually invited Tommy Docherty to our next league game to run the rule over Rangers and analyse what was going wrong; the very same Tommy Docherty who had rubbished me during the home internationals of 1976. It wasn't only Docherty whom the *Mail* called on. Former Rangers manager Scot Symon was wheeled out to explain what Jock 'was going through'.

The *Mail* should have saved its money. Away to Partick Thistle, we won convincingly by four goals to nil, with Jock's new signing Gordon Smith grabbing a double. Despite such a convincing victory Docherty said in his piece that although the team had 'an abundance of talent' it was not 'being utilised properly'. I have never read so much rubbish in all my life.

Even now Docherty was still trying to row back from what he said about me before that game with England at Hampden. His new version of events was that his remarks had been light-hearted and that he thought I would be an asset to any club because I was in 'the Greig mould'. Sorry Tommy, that doesn't wash.

We beat Celtic 3–2 in our next game in the championship and with a few good wins in League Cup sectional games under our belt the 'crisis' at Ibrox was well and truly over. In fact after the win over Thistle in August we went on a long, unbeaten run that took us up to December, when we once again lost heavily to the team that were our closest challengers that season, Aberdeen. One game in particular from those days sticks in my mind: a 4–1 away win against an excellent Motherwell team. We scored four without reply in the first half, playing some wonderful football. Big DJ got a stunning hat trick, with Gordon Smith also on the score sheet.

I also found time to win another treble. But for bowls, not football. In October 1977, at a ceremony held in Stonehouse bowling club, I was presented with the Club trophy, the President's trophy and a cup for winning the pairs championship. It gave me almost as much satisfaction as winning cups and titles with Rangers.

Our great run in the league included a quite incredible Ne'erday Old Firm game at Ibrox. We won quite easily by three goals to one and in so doing left Celtic's title challenge stone dead. But that isn't what makes it stick in the memory. We were leading by a Gordon Smith goal with Celtic pressing hard for an equaliser. During an attack Colin Jackson and Celtic's Joe Craig were jostling in the box. Craig went down after what looked like a nudge from Bomber. The ref, John Gordon, took a good look and decided not to give a penalty, signalling instead that it was a goal kick.

Cue pandemonium.

The Celtic players swarmed round Mr Gordon, jostling him and protesting furiously. He waved them away but, consumed by a sense of injustice, they kept on complaining, not realising, or perhaps even caring, that we intended to carry on with the game. Our keeper, Stewart Kennedy, took the goal kick and after a sweeping move – helped by the absence of the disputatious Celtic players – the ball arrived at the feet of John Greig, who slotted it home.

Celtic's mood darkened even further. In fact they refused to kick-off, booting the ball off the centre spot on three separate occasions. In the meantime their fans, equally enraged, began to throw cans and bottles onto the field. Jock Stein was going crazy on the touchline, urging them to restart the game, and when that failed he sent trainer Neilly Mochan onto the pitch to tell them to get on with it. Fortunately, Mochan was able to persuade them, which was just as well because Mr Gordon confirmed later that he was about to abandon the game, with God-knows-what consequences for the casualty departments of Glasgow's hospitals.

I think the Celtic players were well out of order. I know they were having a terrible season, and that their cause had not been helped by the summer transfer of Kenny Dalglish to Liverpool or by a long-term injury to Danny McGrain.[28] But they knew only too well how combustible Old Firm games can be and they could so easily have provoked a riot that afternoon. Most observers agreed they were in the wrong and one columnist, John Fairgrieve, argued that they had treated the game, the referee and their club with contempt. I couldn't agree more and I am sorry to see that even today, well into the twenty-first century, Celtic are still convinced, for whatever reason, that referees are against them. Paranoia is alive and well and living in the east end of Glasgow.

There was a lot of crowd trouble that season. We were at Fir Park in March 1978, where, after losing two early goals, we hit back with five in a row to take a 5–2 lead. Then a Motherwell player made a gesture to our fans, provoking a hail of bottles and cans. The ref took the players off for five minutes until order was restored. Although we ran out 5–3 winners there was a clamour to replay the game, which even got some backing from the SFA. Willie Waddell was furious and protested in the strongest possible terms. Eventually, the result stood.

In the title race we had a titanic battle with Aberdeen. After the New Year win over Celtic we were six points clear but a stunning 3–0 win for them at Ibrox in March, a defeat to Celtic at Parkhead and too

---

[28] In fact Celtic finished fifth in the Premier Division that season, having been third bottom after we beat them in the New Year game.

many drawn games allowed the Dons to go top in early April. We needed to get a grip and we did. Thanks to three wins on the trot we were able to go into the last game – against Motherwell at Ibrox – with a single-point advantage. Roared on by a big crowd we clinched the club's thirty-seventh league title, courtesy of goals from Colin Jackson and Gordon Smith.

But we were not finished yet. Not by a long chalk. The League Cup was already in the bag. On 18 March we had beaten Celtic 2–1 at Hampden to win the first trophy of the season. Now a second treble in three years loomed large. All we had to do was to put one over on our old adversaries Aberdeen at Hampden Park on 6 May.

They had already beaten us four times during the season, once in the League Cup sectional games and three times in the championship. Time for a bit of payback. Luckily, our team that afternoon at Hampden was formidable, one of the strongest I have ever played in.

Rangers: McCloy, Jardine, Jackson, Forsyth, Greig, Russell, MacDonald, McLean, Johnstone, Smith, Cooper

That outfit had a bit of everything: power, skill, pace, prowess in the air. Aberdeen were in for a tough afternoon on a ground we considered our second home, having already played there three times during the campaign.

Sure enough we were terrific. The 2–1 score line doesn't tell the full story. We were streets ahead of them and goals from Alex MacDonald and Derek Johnstone were the least we deserved. Aberdeen got a late consolation with five minutes to go but that's all it was, a consolation. Bobby Russell, at the age of twenty, was outstanding and was named man of the match.

I was of course delighted to have won another treble but I was even more pleased for Big Jock. He had proved beyond any reasonable doubt that he was a great manager and had put the daft buggers calling for his head at the start of the season well and truly in their place. Not only had he won a glorious treble but also he had become the first Rangers manager in history to win a second treble (prompting one pundit, John Fairgrieve, to pen a column arguing that 'it', by which he meant another Rangers treble, must not happen again for some time because monopolies are bad for the game). It had been a wonderful season apart from another disappointing European campaign but now we had the biggest prize of all to aim at, the European Cup.[29]

I firmly believed that with a man like Jock Wallace at the helm the sky was now the limit. I was sure that with Europe in mind he would strengthen the team again in the summer of 1978 and if he could find three more gems like Smith, Russell and Cooper we could challenge at home and abroad. But what none of us realised was that within the dignified, marbled halls of Ibrox there was acrimony and division.

Our world was to change forever.

---

[29] We went into the European Cup Winners Cup in 1977/78, as a result of being losing finalists in the 1977 Scottish Cup final. Although we knocked out Swiss side Young Boys of Berne in the preliminary round we succumbed to Twente Enschede of Holland in the first-round proper.

15

Off the Park

I was just about to put a juicy piece of fillet steak in my mouth when I heard a voice behind me.

'Excuse me Mr Forsyth can I have your autograph?'

I was sitting in the Reo Stakis steak house in the middle of Glasgow with Linda and our two daughters, Karen and Julie. I don't remember the exact date but it wasn't that long after I signed for Rangers. We had gone for a day's shopping in the city and had decided to finish off with a quiet meal before going back to Stonehouse.

Pretty soon autograph-hunter number one was joined by another Rangers fan, then another. A queue built up at our table, all of them looking to get my signature on menus, napkins, Marks and Spencer receipts, whatever scraps of paper they could lay their hands on. I was taken aback by the attention. It was my first expedition to Glasgow with my family as a Rangers player and I couldn't believe the reaction. After that we stayed closer to home when we dined out.

In Stonehouse everyone knew everyone else and had done since childhood. For the most part they never treated us any differently, although after I signed for Rangers Linda noticed that when she was out shopping more people would approach her.

'How is big Tam doing? I saw him playing for Rangers last week,' they would say.

In their own quiet way I think my friends and neighbours were very proud that I played for Rangers and of course Scotland.

Living in Stonehouse meant that I could escape from the pressures at Ibrox by absorbing myself in my other game: bowls. I have been a member of Stonehouse bowling club for nearly forty years and I am proud to say that I have been club champion on three occasions (the last time in 2006) and a beaten finalist on three others.

My other hobby is gardening. My dad developed a market garden at the back of our house and grew a range of vegetables and flowers, which he would proudly display at the Stonehouse horticultural show. I suppose I inherited his green fingers. It started as a hobby but when my playing days were over it became a good way for me to make a living. I enjoy seeing plants grow. It gives me an enormous sense of satisfaction when those seeds develop into a beautiful chrysanthemum or rose. Linda always says she is amazed at how patient I am when it comes to gardening, considering I have such a short fuse normally!

During my years at Rangers we were, in financial terms, what I would describe as fairly comfortable. When I signed in 1972 my father-in-law did the negotiating, simply because there were very few if any agents in those days. He declined to accept the first offer from Messrs Waddell and Wallace and managed to get them to bump it up to a basic wage of £90 per week, plus bonuses, and a signing-on fee of £1,000.

People will probably think that the wages paid to Rangers players in those days were incredibly low. At the peak of my Ibrox career the most I ever earned in a single season, including bonuses, was around £20,000. Today the top guys expect that and more for a week's work. But for the time it was a good salary. In addition I got a match fee – and potentially a bonus – any time I pulled on the dark-blue jersey of Scotland. So we were really quite well off.

When we first got married we bought my grandmother's terraced house in Stonehouse for a very reasonable price. It was a nice property with a lounge and three bedrooms. However, when I signed on at Ibrox the higher wages enabled me to buy a very nice detached villa, also in Stonehouse and conveniently situated close to the bowling club.

It was a good life, a quiet life for the most part and I can honestly say that despite being a Rangers player for ten years I never got any real hassle from Celtic fans. I must admit it did cross my mind when I signed that I might have a few problems, especially when I remembered what happened to me at the age of seventeen. It was after the 1966 Old Firm Scottish Cup final[30] when I was coming out of Hampden. I saw several Rangers fans lying on the ground covered in blood. Seconds later I was walking past a group of Celtic fans. I had no idea if they were involved in the assault on the Rangers boys but as I went past one of them elbowed me in the face. I was on my own so I had no option but to keep my mouth shut, grit my teeth and keep going.

However, that incident was, I am glad to say, not a sign of things to come. As a Ranger I was hardly Mr Popular with the Celtic fans. I had scored *that* goal in the 1973 Scottish Cup final and of course I had been on the receiving end of severe criticism from the Celtic management for my alleged rough play in a couple of Old Firm games. But off the pitch I got very little abuse, which was no doubt helped by the fact that I lived in Stonehouse (which apart from everyone knowing me so well is primarily what I would call a Rangers town) and kept myself to myself away from football. There is only one other incident I can recall. I had gone for a pint to the Old Ship pub in Stonehouse with a pal and when we got there we found ourselves in the company of a coach-load of Celtic fans on their way back from a game at Kilmarnock. One of them – a guy with a massive scar on his face that he probably didn't get by cutting himself shaving – was clearly not amused at having to share the pub with a Rangers player and he started to give me the evil eye. I knew that the mix of drink and Old Firm rivalry could easily become combustible and when he continued staring at me I began to get a little concerned. But the day was saved by one of his mates, who sidled up to me and asked:

'What do you want to drink?'

'Thanks a lot, but I'm okay,' I replied.

But his offer was not entirely friendly, as he explained.

'I'm not offering because you play for that lot. It's because you play for Scotland.'

---

[30] Rangers won the cup after a replay, in which Kai Johansen notched the only goal of the game with a twenty-five-yard screamer.

Although he never bought me a drink his decision to come up and talk to me seemed to defuse the tension and I was able to enjoy my pint in peace.

* * *

Another important aspect of life at Rangers was the number of games we were expected to take part in, both at home and abroad. It was a hectic schedule, which often left little time for our long-suffering wives and children. There were pre-season friendlies, the Glasgow Cup, the Drybrough Cup, European ties, close-season tours, ad hoc games during the season; not to mention the three domestic competitions. You couldn't coast in the friendly matches, simply because of the quality of the opposition. In my time at Ibrox we faced many top clubs, the likes of Manchester United, Everton, Werder Bremen and Barcelona. Then, for many of us, there were competitive games with Scotland, as well as tours and friendlies.

I think 1975/76 is a good example. The previous campaign had ended with Rangers embarking on a punishing eight-game, end-of-season tour in Canada, New Zealand and Australia (I played in only three of the games) that ended as late as 22 June 1975. Quite astonishingly, we stopped off in Vancouver, Canada on the way out and played a game against a local team before getting back on a New Zealand-bound plane a day later. If memory serves me right we needed eleven flights to complete our itinerary as we endlessly criss-crossed the Antipodes, playing matches in venues as far apart as Christchurch in New Zealand and Perth in Western Australia.

Then, when we finally got back home, we were granted a few short weeks to recover before reporting back for pre-season training in July. There was a friendly against St Mirren on 1 August followed by another against Hertha Berlin three days later before the competitive action kicked off with the League Cup sectional ties on 9 August. We managed to win the domestic treble that year, and also competed in the European Cup, so every game we played was high intensity. The season ended for me with three ties in the home internationals in May 1976 before I got on a plane for a tour of North America with Rangers, in which I took part in all five games.

Some people go on about the easy lives that footballers enjoy but when you are pushing your body to the limit sixty or seventy times a year it takes a toll. And that is doubly true when the flights to far-off places are taken into account. I think it was Bill Shankly who said that long plane journeys have the same effect on players as sugar does on a petrol tank.

So we needed our holidays, not just to give us some much-needed time with our families but also to recharge the batteries. And there is no doubt Linda and I had some great holidays, often in the company of friends like Tommy and Beth McLean and Peter and Anne McCloy. Spain was a favourite and one year we went to Tenerife with Peter and Anne and the next year to Majorca with Tommy and Beth. The Majorca trip nearly ended in tragedy when yours truly tried to do an impression of Ian 'the Torpedo' Thorpe, the great Australian swimmer. I had always hated swimming but when I picked up a pelvic injury Rangers sent me to Larkhall baths to take exercise in the pool. After a while I began to feel more confident in the water so when I got to the Balearics I was ready for a few lengths in the hotel swimming pool.

Or so I thought.

Linda, Tommy and Beth had decided to take it easy and were lazing on sun-beds in an area about fifty yards from the pool. But I wasn't having any of that so I took a running jump into the shallow end of the pool. But instead of tiles below my feet all I could feel was more and more water. I had jumped into the deep end. When I realised where I was, my new-found confidence instantly evaporated. I panicked and began bobbing up and down like a man possessed. You will have heard the old saying 'not waving but drowning', well that was me. I tried my best to shout 'help' as I jumped up and down in the water but nothing came out of my mouth. After flailing around for what seemed an eternity, I managed to grab the edge of the pool and hauled myself out.

'I nearly drowned,' I told my three sunbathing companions, who had been completely oblivious to my predicament. Did I get I get any sympathy? You must be joking. They nearly killed themselves laughing at my stupidity. I can assure you that that was the last swim I tried on that particular holiday.

While holidays in the sun are all very well, to us they didn't compare to the times we had on the wonderful island of Arran, or 'Scotland in Miniature' as it is often known. I have always loved this beautiful place and have returned to it again and again over the years. Linda and I bought a residential caravan in Lamlash with my sister Margaret and her husband in 1974 to give us somewhere to take our growing family, and later we bought our own caravan on the same site. We enjoyed many wonderful family holidays there.

I think we went there for about ten years, and even today we occasionally go back to visit. Many are the times that Peter and Tommy and their families came across. In some ways we were an unusual trio: Peter is six foot four, I am about six while Tommy is just five foot six. Not for nothing did we remind people of that famous routine on *The Frost Report* with John Cleese, Ronnie Barker and Ronnie Corbett. We were never short of visitors in Arran. Even Gordon Smith and his wife Marlene made the trip and we were so short of space that they had to sleep on the floor. I know that will surprise many people: Gordon Smith – that smooth, well-dressed man about town – roughing it in an overcrowded caravan but that was the effect Arran had on people. We all mucked in, had fun and made the best of it.

It was a real family atmosphere. We put on the Lamlash Superstars, named after the popular BBC programme of the time. We would compete in golf, tennis, bowling, pool, snooker and Boggle (a word game). I hate to brag but I usually won the male Superstar trophy while my sister invariably won the female version. I took Superstars seriously, probably too seriously, and I wasn't impressed by my wife's tennis technique because every time she hit a good shot she would take a drink of Martini and lemonade. I can't imagine Venus Williams doing that at Wimbledon!

With up to eleven people in our caravan cooking was a real palaver but Linda became a dab hand at feeding the multitudes on a two-burner gas cooker. If the weather was fine we set up our barbecue outside the van and made a night of it. Some people might not realise it but I have always fancied myself as a bit of a singer! After a few refreshments I would belt out my entire repertoire, although Linda will tell you my favourite number from those days was a little ditty entitled 'My Mother-in-Law'. Sometimes big Peter would join me for a duet, which must have been cruel and unusual punishment for our neighbours on the site.

When I wasn't competing in Superstars I was out on Lamlash's hilly golf course at eight o' clock in the morning, competing in a sweep. The wives and children would arrive at lunchtime and we would either have something to eat in the clubhouse or take a picnic to the beach. One day we went on an outing to Shiskine golf club in the company of members from the Lamlash golf club. When I came off the course I walked across to the Rock hotel, just a few steps from the clubhouse. It was half-past two, way after closing time, but as I was desperate for a pint I decide to try my luck with the elderly barman.

'What time do you shut the bar?' I asked in a rather hopeful tone of voice.

'October, son.'

That was Arran to a tee. Sod the rules and regulations and let's have a good time.

Even today when I get together with Peter and Tommy and Gordon and our wives we always reminisce about the old times on Scotland in Miniature.

Happy days indeed.

16

It Still Haunts Me: Argentina 1978

I still think about Argentina every day. It doesn't matter where I am or what I am doing: at work, in the house, playing bowls, babysitting the grandkids. It haunts me. It really does. People have gone over and over what happened, putting forward this theory and that theory. They bring up the stories about indiscipline, drinking and the rows about bonuses, all of which were complete nonsense, but unfortunately did nothing for squad harmony when they were aired in public. They cite Ally's lack of experience and professionalism, which sadly were all too true. They refer to the poor training facilities and the dingy accommodation, again undeniable. They recall the unprecedented media hype and the ill-conceived send-off at Hampden, all of it unwise. They rehash the Willie Johnston affair, which was hardly a help. But there was another good reason for the debacle of '78.

We, the players, didn't do our job on the field of play.

You can analyse the three games against Peru, Iran and Argentina till the cows come home but the fact is that we should have qualified from that section and gone on to make a mark in the tournament. It was there for the taking. We were good enough, no question. The off-field problems and the manager's inadequacies certainly didn't help but we should have been professional enough to put them out of our minds and to concentrate on the job in hand.

But let's go back to the day that marked the start of our campaign to win the World Cup: 14 January 1978. That was when the draw was made in the San Martin theatre in Buenos Aires. Ally MacLeod was there and when Scotland was placed in the same group as Peru, Iran and Holland he thought all his Christmases had come at once, as, it must be acknowledged, did the Scotland players and the entire Scottish nation.[31] Ally later proclaimed it a dream section, arguing that by the time Scotland came to play Holland both countries would have qualified courtesy of easy wins over Peru and Iran. He also went on to disparage Peru's leading players as 'old men', and was particularly critical of star forward Teofilo Cubillas, whom he described as tubby and ageing. But what no one ever mentioned was that Cubillas was only twenty-nine (and a former South American player of the year) or that Peru were the reigning South American champions having taken the scalps of many top sides along the way, including Brazil.[32]

From that moment on the hysteria built. Ally was never off our television screens, telling anyone who would listen that we had a great chance of winning if not the World Cup then at least a medal. The man's enthusiasm was infectious. He had us all believing that we were destined for great things, that we were world beaters, that all we had to do was turn up. A more experienced manager, a Jock Stein or a Jock Wallace, would never have gone down that road. It was disrespectful to the opposition and, even more importantly, guaranteed to fire them up.

Not that Ally was alone in his delusions of grandeur. Many in the media, including some very experienced journalists, argued that we had a great chance of winning the tournament, an argument that many players and fans bought into. I think that whole period is summed up by Andy Cameron's hit 'Ally's Tartan Army', which got to number six in the charts. It was a ridiculously over-the-top song that talked about shaking people up when Scotland won the World Cup.

---

[31] A practice draw had placed Scotland alongside Brazil, France and Austria so perhaps Ally's euphoria was in fact relief.

[32] In 2004 Cubillas was named one of FIFA's 125 best living footballers, in a list compiled by Pele. He is also the highest-scoring midfielder in the history of the World Cup finals, with ten goals. With more than five hundred goals, he is recognised as Peru's greatest player. Truly a class act.

We got a timely warning in the home internationals, a competition we had dominated during the previous two years. Despite playing all three games at Hampden – and drawing an incredible 222,000 fans – we failed to win any of them. The biggest disappointment was against England. We had the lion's share of possession, but just couldn't score and lost 1–0 thanks to a goal from Stevie Coppell. In a sign of what was to come Ally persevered with Joe Jordan and Kenny Dalglish, who both had poor games by their own high standards, when he should have brought on Derek Johnstone, a striker in form as his goal against Northern Ireland the week before showed. It was my first taste of defeat against our oldest enemy and it was not one I relished. Alarm bells should have been ringing: after a long, successful run we had gone off the boil just a few weeks before the biggest tournament on earth. But no one seemed to realise it and we made one blunder after another.

One of those blunders was Ally's failure to watch either Peru or Iran. Whether this was because he didn't rate them or because of the distances involved I have no idea. I think most players would agree the more that you know about your opponents the easier your job is. It's not as if he was overworked. Between qualification in October 1977 and the home internationals in May 1978 we only had one game, a friendly against Bulgaria at Hampden. That gave him a great opportunity to spy on our future opponents but, unfortunately, it was one that he passed up.

There was a carnival atmosphere surrounding the squad, even in our pre-tournament training camp in Dunblane. Celebrities popped in to wish us luck on a regular basis, and although it was fun at the time and great copy for the papers with hindsight it was something of a distraction. I remember Rod Stewart arrived this day to wish us luck and have a bit of a kick-about with the lads. He had been a promising youth player and had trials with several professional clubs in the London area. So the manager organised a bounce game, with Rod selected for one of the teams. Before kick-off Ally came up to me and gleefully whispered:

'Tam, go and sort him out.'

It would have been a great joke – and a big story for the papers – for the Iron Man of the Scotland team to have crunched into the preening pop star and for a moment I gave it serious consideration.

Then I noticed how skinny Rod's legs were and I realised that if I tackled at full power I would really hurt the guy. So I went easy on him and the journalists had to look elsewhere for a new angle.

Then came what was for me the biggest faux pas of all: the triumphal send-off at Hampden on 25 May 1978. Victory parades come after successful events, not before them. Ally's supporters will argue that the idea for the send-off did not come from him, that it was designed with public safety in mind, but I don't buy that. He had amassed enough credit with both the SFA and the Scottish public to have vetoed it had he so wished. So, whoever was responsible, we players were paraded one by one on the famous Hampden pitch as thirty thousand tartan-clad supporters went mad. I am not blaming just Ally. At the time I thought it was great, as did most of the squad. But I say again: with a more streetwise and experienced man at the helm it wouldn't have happened.

Much has been made of the different way in which the squad on the one hand and the SFA blazers on the other were treated with regard to flights and accommodation. Was there any truth in it? You bet.

When we arrived in Argentina we were sent to Alta Gracia. It was a one-horse town – or it would have been if the said nag hadn't already been sent to the knacker's yard. Our hotel, the Sierras, was a pit; that is the only word I can use to describe it. By British standards it was, at best, a one-star establishment and what made it even worse was that a refurbishment programme was ongoing when we were staying there. The Waldorf Astoria it was not. On the first morning I was walking barefoot across my room when my foot was punctured by a very sharp skelf. Not ideal for international footballers competing in the World Cup finals! When Alan Rough, Sandy Jardine and Derek Johnstone went for a walk they were held at gunpoint by Argentine police, a frightening experience given the political turmoil that the country was going through. The training facilities were just awful, although coming from Scottish football that was something we should have been well used to.

We had one consolation. At least the SFA 'blazerati' and assorted hangers-on were suffering too. Wrong. They were staying in a five-star, luxury hotel in another town. You really couldn't make it up. While the accommodation and training facilities were not responsible for our poor showing in Argentina the way we were treated by the blazerati did cause resentment, and may have been a contributory factor in our performances.

After a few days in Alta Gracia we were stir crazy. The first game against Peru, to be played in a new stadium in Cordoba on 3 June 1978, couldn't come quickly enough.

Scotland: Rough, Kennedy, Forsyth, Burns, Buchan, Rioch, Masson, Hartford, Dalglish, Jordan, Johnston

That team says a lot about Ally McLeod's management style. He was faithful to the guys who got him there, the guys who had done him proud in the past. I understand that. It's human nature. Who wouldn't want to reward the people who had given everything for you in the past? Yet I firmly believe that a stronger, shrewder and more experienced manager would have gone for the men in form, which for me would have meant a midfield berth for Graeme Souness and also a striking spot for Derek Johnstone, if not in the starting eleven, then certainly coming off the bench.

On a personal level it was another great career milestone – playing my first game in the finals of the biggest sporting competition on earth. Just look where all that kicking a ball about on the streets of Stonehouse had got me! I prayed that I would do myself justice.

Everything went well. We flew out of the blocks and put them under immediate pressure, creating a few good chances in the opening ten minutes. The crowd, and the millions watching on television, saw with their own eyes the evidence of Scotland's superiority, and we did nothing to disabuse them of that notion by taking a deserved lead in the fourteenth minute. Bruce Rioch, homing in on goal, unleashed a fine shot, which their keeper, Quironga, could only parry. The ball fell to the feet of Joe Jordan and the big man promptly swept it home.

After the goal we should have gone on to seal the game but we proceeded to miss several excellent opportunities. Then, inevitably, Peru got stronger, pushing us further and further back. They were due a goal and it duly arrived two minutes before half time when Cueto slotted one past Alan Rough. It wasn't that we were playing badly, if anything we dominated the first half; it's just that Peru were much better than we had been led to believe.

In the second half we once again came out all guns blazing, peppering the opposition goal with shots and headers. Quironga however was in inspired form and became the hero of an entire nation when, after sixty-two minutes, he parried a Don Masson penalty kick to safety. The miss inspired them but discomfited us.

They really came into their own, sweeping towards our box with some beautiful passing movements. After one such move the ball arrived at the feet of Cubillas, who controlled it perfectly before stroking it effortlessly into the net.

But Mr Cubillas wasn't finished yet. In the seventy-seventh minute we were penalised for a foul committed a couple of yards outside of our box. We put a pretty solid-looking wall in place and waited for them to do their worst. Four of their guys hovered around the ball, working out who was going to take the free kick. I thought to myself it won't be Cubillas taking it as he is too close the ball and in completely the wrong position. But as the song goes, look how wrong you can be.

The man showed his world-class ability by taking the shortest run-up I have ever seen and nonchalantly flicking the ball into the net. Our world fell apart.

We never recovered from that free kick and Peru ran out winners by three goals to one. I don't think we played all that badly. In fact we had more of the play and more chances than them. It was just that we came up against someone I can only describe as a superstar, and a superstar at the top of his game. He was the difference between the two teams. Perhaps if we had known more about Cubillas we could have taken the appropriate action in terms of tactics and marking. Perhaps we would have played with more urgency knowing how good he and his teammates actually were. No modern manager would have gone into such an important game without having watched the opposition and then briefing his players. Either Ally genuinely thought we would be too good for them or he just couldn't be bothered to make the effort. But whether he was naive or lazy, or a combination of both, he let us down, no question about it.

But no matter the qualities of the opposition it was the lowest point of my career, something I have been trying to come to terms with ever since. I had hit rock bottom. At that moment I just wanted to get in a taxi, drive to the airport and get on the first plane home. Defeat was especially hard to take because we had been on such a high going into the game. The only consolation was that the next game was just four days later and slowly but surely we got our focus back.

If we could at least hang on to the consolation of a reasonable performance against the Peruvians the same cannot be aid for our display against Iran, the group minnows. I seemed to be one of those who carried the can for the Peru game and was relegated to the bench, although Ally described it as a 'tactical switch'. In the event I did get on, replacing Buchan, who had picked up a knock, in the fifty-third minute.

What an experience it turned out to be!

The 1–1 draw we eked out against the Iranians really was a humiliation. I think the *Daily Record* summed it up perfectly. Under the headline 'Cry for Us, Argentina', it describes us as 'fourth rate', a harsh but unfortunately accurate description of our performance. The Scotland fans, who had paid small fortunes to get there, were incensed, and threw their scarves at us as we trudged disconsolately from the pitch. Every Scotland fan will remember the scenes after the game as we trooped onto the team bus while being regaled with choruses of 'What a load of rubbish' from the Tartan Army. I was shattered. We all were. There may have been an excuse for losing to Peru, a quality side, but Iran were the minnows, the whipping boys of the group.[33] There was of course uproar, both in Argentina and at home. Ally came in for some terrible stick and he aged ten years before our eyes. Reflecting the bitter disappointment of a nation I heard that his children were getting a really hard time at school.

Amazingly enough, even after two such bitter disappointments, we could still qualify, provided we could beat the Dutch by three clear goals. Talk about the proverbial mountain to climb. But, inspired by a great performance by Graeme Souness (who took his rightful place in the side, albeit belatedly) we nearly pulled it off and when wee Archie Gemmill scored that wonder goal to make it 3–1 we were in

---

[33] They were certainly the whipping boys for our main group opponents. Peru beat the Iranians 4–1 (with Cubillas getting a hat-trick) while Holland recorded an easy 3–0 win.

dreamland. I actually had a chance to make it 4–1: from a corner I got my head on the ball about six yards out but sent it just past the post. If I had scored it would have made for a very interesting last fifteen minutes. Of course we all know what happened next: Holland scored a stunning goal from long range to make it 3–2, which was how the game and our participation in the 1978 World Cup ended.

It was a great win. After all Holland were one of the pre-tournament favourites and would go on to reach the final, in which they lost narrowly to hosts Argentina. But it was much too little and it was much too late. We were going home and we were going home with our tails between our legs.

The return journey was made even more uncomfortable by the bigwigs at the SFA. In Buenos Aires, waiting for our flight back to the UK, we were put up overnight in a hotel. I use the word 'hotel' loosely because the place was little better than a doss-house. If you remember the Great Eastern hotel in Glasgow – home to generations of tramps, alkies and other unfortunates – you will get some idea of what this place was like. When I went up to my room I turned on the tap in the wash-hand basin and rust came out! I know we had played badly in the World Cup but this was most definitely cruel and unusual punishment. Buchan was one of the first to complain and then we all weighed in. Eventually, the SFA relented and we got taken to the Buenos Aires Sheraton. We had gone from no stars to five stars.

Although the players won that skirmish the battle was far from over. The blazers were still determined to teach us a lesson and on the plane home we found out just how petty they could be. While we were booked into economy, the officials all had seats in first class. Given that the whole party travelled first class on the way out this could only have been a punishment for our failure to qualify for the second stage of the competition. It was par for the course. They saw us as second-class citizens and made sure we got seats to match that status.

* * *

Even now, more than thirty years later, I regularly mull over what happened in Argentina. I am still looking for answers. Many informed observers have argued that the Scotland squad was the best ever to leave the shores of the British Isles. We certainly had players of genuine class: Dalglish, Souness, Jordan, McQueen, Johnston, Hartford, Gemmill and many others besides. Despite a blip in the home internationals that immediately preceded Argentina the results achieved by that same group of players had been very impressive.

So what went wrong?

I believe there were three reasons for our failure in Argentina. The first was the level of organisation and planning. In my view the SFA did not put enough time and effort into either. Why were we stuck in a dump like Alta Gracia in a rundown hotel with inadequate training facilities, especially when the officials who ran our game were staying in the lap of luxury? That created disharmony and got the whole enterprise off to the worst possible start.

The second factor was Ally. He was a nice guy, a football enthusiast, a man who dared a nation to believe, but also naive and hopelessly out of his depth in the hothouse of the World Cup finals. Worse still he got swept away by the hype he himself did so much to generate, leading him to conclude that preparation was strictly for ordinary mortals. A more experienced manager, someone who had dealt successfully with high-expectation levels, would have made us all see sense. Jock Stein was the favourite for the job before Ally was appointed but for one reason or another he turned it down. He would have been ideal as would Jock Wallace, both forged in the white-hot heat of the Old Firm fire.

Nor to be frank would I give Ally very high marks for his technical skills. He had little interest either in tactics or in analysing the style of play practised by our opponents. He also persevered with players who had done a job for him in the past, even when they had clearly lost form. There was a strong case for playing Graeme Souness against Peru, an even stronger one for playing him from the start against Iran. Yet he waited until the Holland game when we were almost down and out before giving him a place. That was a mistake.

I also believe he got it wrong about Derek Johnstone. I realise big DJ was not everyone's cup of tea. His work-rate wasn't at the same level as that of Jordan or Dalglish. But the guy was a fantastic goal-scorer and he was particularly strong in the air. He had also scored forty-plus times for Rangers in 1977/78 and was instrumental in us winning the domestic treble. It was no surprise that he was named player of the year by the football writers and by his fellow professionals a few months before the finals.

What more do you have to do to get a game for Scotland?

But Ally wouldn't even bring him on as a sub. I know that Derek and the manager were far from bosom buddies but when the nation's hopes are riding on the result you have to swallow your pride and go for the guy who is most likely to grab a goal.

Finally, I must point the finger at myself and the other players. Could we have given more, despite the difficulties caused by the lack of organisation and the poor preparation? Yes, we should have done better. There is no getting away from it; we didn't do ourselves, or the Scottish people, justice.

And for that I apologise.

17

Decline and Fall: the John Greig Years

They say it never rains but it pours. That was certainly true of the summer of 1978. Not long after I got back home from Argentina I got a phone call that was to change my professional life forever. It was John Greig who rang. He told me Jock Wallace had left Ibrox and that he had been made manager of Rangers.

I had a strong sense of personal loss. Not only had big Jock made me his first signing but also he had always backed me when the going got tough. I don't know why he left when he did. Some say it was because he wanted a higher salary, others that the board wouldn't give him a big enough transfer budget. Perhaps it was a combination of the two. I am sure that Jock would have had his reasons. He was an honourable man and I just don't think he would have walked unless he truly believed that he was being unfairly treated or that the team would suffer because of lack of investment. We will probably never know for certain.

Whatever the reason for his departure, it was in my view a retrograde step. The man had worked wonders at Rangers. Apart from winning two trebles in three seasons he had stopped Celtic doing ten in a row, lifted the centenary Scottish Cup and had played a major part in Rangers winning the European Cup Winners Cup in Barcelona. He was Rangers through and through and would often tell the players that if you cut him he would bleed blue blood. Experience, commitment, success: what more could any club want in a manager?

If he had stayed and had been able to get the new players he wanted I am sure Rangers would have gone on to scale even greater heights. But even though we had just won a treble and were just 3/1 to win another one in 1978/79 (Celtic were 33/1 to achieve the same feat) the team did need new blood, especially if we were to compete at the sharp end of the European Cup, which I am sure is where Jock envisaged us being. Many of his stalwarts – including me – were in our late twenties, early thirties and an injection of younger blood would have given the whole club a lift.

Instead we got John Greig. Based on his record as a player I think everyone thought at the time it was a good appointment. As a Rangers supporter I had looked up to the man since boyhood. He gave everything for that light-blue jersey and I even remember him, towards the end of games, kicking the ball over the stand at Fir Park if Rangers were winning just to waste a few valuable seconds. He was without doubt the most committed player I have ever come across during my time in professional football.

On a personal level I had always got on well with John. He was a nice guy who had helped me to settle into the dressing room after my move from Motherwell. I remember one time when I was injured he took me to see a doctor he had consulted about his own injury. So while I would have preferred big Jock still to have been in place at least his replacement was someone I knew and could respect. It might even be the start of a glorious new era for Rangers.

Sadly, I got that one completely wrong.

John Greig had an excellent grasp of tactics but he did not have the experience to manage Rangers. To go straight from being a player, no matter how great, to the manager's office at one of the biggest clubs in the world is a step too far. Players would have run through a brick wall for Jock Wallace but from what I saw John Greig did not inspire that same level of passion. In addition his personality seemed to change when he became manager. He became, it seemed to me, aloof, mistrustful and a bearer of grudges, not ideal traits for getting the best out of eleven highly trained athletes.

It wasn't that Greig was a complete disaster as Rangers manager. I would characterise his reign as one of gradual decline: a decline in results, in the quality of players, in the standard of football we played. He did have his successes, no question. In his first season we won two cup competitions, starting with the League Cup, in which we defeated Celtic in the semis, then a strong Aberdeen side, with the likes of Strachan, Miller, Archibald and Harper in its ranks, in the final. In May the team added the Scottish Cup, beating Hibs 3–2 in a replayed final after the first game had ended in a goalless draw. Unfortunately, I missed both games in what was a depressing, injury-hit season that saw me go under the knife for an operation on the cartilage in my right knee.

In the league we made an awful start, winning only one of our opening nine games. But we recovered and even gave ourselves a realistic chance of winning the title. However, it was too little too late and our chances evaporated on an infamous night at Celtic Park when our Old Firm rivals beat us 4–2 despite being reduced to ten men. We finished second, three points behind Celtic, but I feel that we could easily have won another treble had it not been for a momentous decision made by John Greig about Derek Johnstone's position in the team.

Although DJ had scored thirty-nine times in 1977/78 when playing as a striker, and had also been named player of the year, he had made no secret of his desire to move back to centre half. That, to me at least, made no sense at all. Goal-scorers of his calibre are like gold dust; they are almost impossible to replace, especially with guys like Billy Urquhart, who, with all due respect, simply wasn't in the same class. I know that Derek had been agitating for more money and had put in a transfer request so perhaps accommodating him at the back was part of the deal. He was also made captain of the team, another decision I found baffling when you consider we had guys with more obvious leadership skills, not least Sandy Jardine and Alex MacDonald. I believed – and I wasn't the only one in the dressing room who felt this way – Johnstone had been pandered to, that he had been given favoured status by Greig.

But it was the decision to play him in the centre of defence that really hurt the team. Although he did occasionally turn out as a striker, and also as a midfielder, his goal tally plummeted from thirty-nine in 1977/78 to fifteen in 1978/79, while the team could manage only fifty-two goals in thirty-six league games compared to seventy-six in the same number of games the year before. I believe Greig's momentous decision cost us the league – and a treble. I couldn't help reflecting on how Jock Wallace would have handled the situation. He would have dismissed Derek's request out of hand and he would have been right to do so. A manager is not put on earth to please his players. He is there to take the right decision for the only thing that matters: the team. In my view Greig didn't have the strength of character to take the right – as opposed to the popular – decision and in consequence we all suffered.

Perhaps our most impressive performances that season came in the European Cup. In the first round we were drawn against Juventus, the favourites for the competition and one of the most formidable teams in Europe. No one gave us a chance and when you look at their team, managed by the legendary Giovanni Trapattoni, you could understand why. They had a host of world-class players, guys like Zoff, Gentile, Cabrini, Bettega and Tardelli. In fact six members of that Juventus team would play for the Italy side that won the 1982 World Cup in Spain. The press also noted that Rangers had never knocked out an Italian team in European competition.

But to give him his due John got his tactics spot on for the first leg in the Stadio Comunale in Turin. He gave Sandy Jardine a new role as sweeper leaving Bomber Jackson and I to man mark their strikers, Bettega and Virdis. It worked a treat and despite losing a early goal there was no further scoring. The return at Ibrox was without doubt one of the highlights of my time at Rangers. All of our experienced guys played superbly that night, from Sandy Jardine to Tommy McLean and Alex MacDonald to Gordon Smith. Wee Doddy got the first and, fittingly, Gordon Smith got the winner. I say fittingly because Smudger had been the victim of a horrific tackle by Benetti in the first leg, a tackle that had it been an inch lower would have broken his leg.

It was a massive victory for everyone connected with the club and an undoubted personal triumph for Greig. Indeed some would argue that it was the best result ever achieved by a Rangers team in Europe, considering the quality of the opposition. It was all the more amazing considering that when we played the second leg on 27 September 1978 we had yet to win a league game.

If we thought the draw for the next round would be kinder we were very much mistaken. PSV Eindhoven – the UEFA Cup holders and another team awash with top international players – were to be our opponents. This time the first leg was at home and although we played some excellent football we missed a hatful of chances and the game finished goalless. Although we had not conceded an away goal few pundits gave us much of a chance in the return, especially as PSV would be at full strength having been forced to play an injury-weakened eleven at Ibrox.

Once again we proved the pundits wrong. The manager had undertaken an extensive study of the opposition and he got his tactics spot on. We lost an early goal but inspired by Bobby Russell – who probably had his best ever game in a Rangers shirt – we won by three goals to two. It was fitting that Bobby got the third goal, a wonderful curling shot after a magnificent pass from Tommy McLean. The reception we got from our fans when we flew back into Glasgow was quite exceptional and the media too were effusive, with some papers even arguing that we were now favourites to win the European Cup, given that we had eliminated two of the favourites. We had undoubtedly done well but that, I thought at the time, was going a bit too far.

It is certainly true that the draw could have been a bit kinder. After facing the champions of Italy and Holland we were pitched in against Cologne in the quarter-finals. This was an outstanding side that had won the West German league-and-cup double during the previous season and had players of the calibre of Harald Schumacher, Pierre Littbarski and Bernd Schuster, all of whom would play prominent parts in the 1982 World Cup finals. Despite their undoubted quality I still fancied us to beat them over two legs.

The fact is that we just didn't get a rub of the green in that tie. Older readers will remember the winter of 1978/79. It was the worst cold snap of the twentieth century, with Carnwath in my native Lanarkshire recording an incredible temperature of minus 25 degrees Centigrade. It was so bad, the *Daily Record* reported, that people's specs actually froze over! The result, in the days before under-soil heating, was the mass postponement of football matches. In fact between 23 December 1978 and 20 January 1979 Rangers did not play a single game and even after that, as the cold spell continued to exert its icy grip, games were sporadic right up until April.

In consequence, when we took to the field in Cologne on 6 March 1979 we were sadly lacking in match practice. Our other problem was injuries. We went into those ties missing several key players, including Derek Johnstone. Despite that we gave a good account of ourselves, losing by the only goal of the game in Germany and then drawing 1–1 at Ibrox. It was a sad end to what could have been a glorious run, one that could have taken us to the final with Nottingham Forest. It is one of my great regrets that despite scaling the heights with Rangers on the domestic scene, and playing for Scotland in the World Cup finals, I did not get to a European final.

18

My Worst-Ever Season

After the triumphs of the Jock Wallace years I sensed that as season 1979/80 loomed the club's fortunes were on a downward spiral. There seemed to be little money to spend at a time when new blood was badly needed to freshen up a side whose most prominent members – Peter McCloy, Derek Johnstone, Alex MacDonald, Sandy Jardine and myself – were either on the wrong side of thirty or not a kick in the arse from that milestone. Our last big moves in the transfer market had been the signings of Gordon Smith and Davie Cooper, but they were two years previously. With the reconstruction of Ibrox costing the club an arm and a leg there was very little left for team building, although a stronger and more experienced manager might have been able to squeeze more out of the board.

Greig's argument – at least in public – was that were there many talented young players at Ibrox and they had to be given a chance to shine. Fair enough, but the problem was that the new batch of young-sters – the Billy Urquharts, the Gordon Dalziels, the Billy MacKays, the Derek Stricklands – weren't, with all due respect to them, any-where near the standard of the stalwarts they hoped to replace. Even when Greig did manage to buy players – for example Gregor Stevens, Colin McAdam and Ian Redford – they never quite hit the heights despite having cost the club a fair amount of money. I also think they suffered by being compared with the greats who had preceded them, the likes of Johnston, Jardine, MacDonald, Jackson and Greig himself.[34] I do have to admit that John got one signing right: the capture of Jim Bett was a shrewd move and it is just a pity he didn't stay at Ibrox for longer.

For me the new season started as the old one had ended: in misery. I had been out since March 1979 due to a severe problem with the cartilage in my right knee and had hoped to make my return in a Drybrough Cup tie against Berwick Rangers at the end of July. But, to my dismay, the knee had not healed and I found myself on the sidelines yet again, a situation that would persist until December. Every player hates being out and I was no exception.

The first part of the league campaign was truly awful for Rangers. We lost seven of our first fifteen games, winning only five, and by the end of November we were joint second bottom of the table after sustaining three defeats in a row. That dismal run included a comfortable 3–1 win for newly promoted Dundee at Dens Park, a result that prompted chants of 'Greig must go' from the travelling Rangers fans.

I made my long-awaited comeback from injury on 2 December 1979 – along with my fellow crock, Bobby Russell – and it seemed to help. We won three games in a row, and hauled ourselves up to third place in the league. Unfortunately, however, we couldn't sustain it and after that we lost as many as we won. In a forgettable sequence of results only one game has stuck in my mind. It was a wild ninety minutes, with some meaty challenges, four bookings and battles on the terracing. Not content with fighting among themselves the fans decided to throw bottles at the players. One of them decided to inject a little levity into the proceedings: he picked up a bottle from the pitch and pretended to drink from it.

His name? George Best. The maestro, in the twilight of a wonderful but troubled career, was by then a Hibs player. He was a little overweight and much slower than in his heyday but still a talent. He helped his team to a 2–1 win that afternoon.

---

34 In 1980 Rangers paid Dundee £210,000 for Redford's services, setting a new record for a transfer between Scottish clubs.

I think season 1979/80 must rank as one of the worst ever for Rangers. We finished fifth in the league, one point above Morton and Partick Thistle, who were in joint sixth place. It left us eleven points behind champions Aberdeen and, incredibly, five points behind St Mirren. And don't forget it was still two points for a win in those days. For a club like Rangers statistics like those are not simply unacceptable, they are practically nightmarish.

It wasn't much better in the cups. The early rounds of the League Cup were based on a two-leg format and after knocking out Clyde we were beaten home and away by Aberdeen in the second round. The Scottish Cup wasn't quite so bad. We got to the final after some excellent performances – including a 6–1 demolition of Hearts, in which yours truly netted an own goal – which set us up for an Old Firm encounter in the hot Hampden sun. The game itself was a scrappy affair in which I was booked early on for a foul on George McCluskey. With defences on top the regulation ninety minutes finished goalless and we moved into extra time. The breakthrough came with 107 minutes on the clock when Danny McGrain fired in a speculative effort from about thirty yards. There is no danger from that distance I thought. And there wasn't, at least until McCluskey instinctively stuck out a leg and diverted the ball past big Peter and into the net. It was a lucky goal and a sickening way to lose a cup final, especially against your oldest rivals.

But it was what happened next that made the game headline news across the world.

At the end of the game, as the Celtic players went to take the applause of their supporters, people lost control of their emotions. A Celtic fan came onto the pitch, ran up to the centre circle and made a gesture to the Rangers fans. And no he wasn't inviting them to go for a pint after the game! Then some Rangers fans clambered over the fence and made their way onto the playing surface. This was followed by a mini invasion of Celtic fans, prompting even more of our fans to follow suit. It didn't take long for the trouble to start. Those idiots chased each other up and down that Hampden pitch, pursued all the while by mounted police desperately trying to get them off the playing surface. Despite the best efforts of the police there was much blood spilt and I suppose it was just sheer good fortune that no one was killed.

Along with some of my teammates I had been shepherded into the dressing room and did not witness what had happened, although I couldn't miss the endless reruns on television in the days and weeks that followed. I think drink had a lot to do with the disorder. It was a very hot day and the fans of both sides had been busy quenching their thirst before the game. Then of course when they got to the stadium many had their traditional 'cairry-oots', most of which were empty by the final whistle. One good thing that came out of that day was that a law was passed making it an offence for drunks, or drink, to be admitted to a stadium.

After a season like that I comforted myself with the thought that things really couldn't get any worse. I was wrong. They could and what happened that summer would spoil my relationship with John Greig forever.

In June 1980 we headed out on tour, to Canada. On the plane journey out, no doubt to the relieve the boredom induced by a long flight, Greig and Derek Johnstone played what they thought was a hilarious practical joke on me. To this day they are convinced that I fell for it. I am afraid however the last laugh is on them.

Anyway, I was sitting there quite content when a stewardess came up to me and said:

'Mr Forsyth. There's a phone call for you. I think it might be a journalist but I'm not really sure.'

I immediately smelt a rat but decided to play along and see where it took me.

'It'll be the wife,' I replied, in a jocular tone.

I got up and went to the station used by the stewardesses, where I was handed an intercom. I knew that there was no way in the world it could be a phone call from Scotland but just to play along with their little game I picked the thing up and asked:

'Hello. Tom Forsyth here. Can I help you?'

In the background I heard either John or Derek say, 'he believes us' and having a good laugh to themselves.

Tam Craig, the club physio, walked past and asked:

'Who is it?'

'It's three reporters,' I replied.

Tam must have told the other passengers in the vicinity I had fallen for it because when I was walking back to my seat they gave me a round of applause. I had never been so embarrassed in my life because I knew they thought I had fallen for it. I have no doubt Messrs Greig and Johnstone thought they had put one over on me. In fact, Greig even told the story of the phantom phone call on the Andy Cameron television show and he also included it in the programme for my testimonial game. A joke is a joke and I have played a few in my time, but in my view going public like that was a deliberate attempt by John to humiliate me.

The incident on the plane soured my relationship with the manager and it was perhaps inevitable that it would not be long before the simmering tensions between us came to the boil. On the tour we played a number of sides from the Continent, including Nancy of France and Ascoli of Italy, and it was during the half-time break against one of them that Greig and I had a right barney over something that happened on the pitch. The opposition had won a corner and decided to play a short one instead of lofting the ball into the box. One of their players then ran towards our goal and simply because Greig had not delegated anyone to cover short corners I ran out and tried to close him down. The upshot was that the ball was thrown into the box but was quickly cleared.

But when I came in at half time John took issue with my decision to leave the box while the corner was being taken. In fact he was raging. His view was that I should have stayed inside the box and marked their striker. For the life of me I couldn't see where he was coming from. I had no real alternative but to go out there because there was a good chance that they would have scored from the corner. I was also annoyed that a couple of his blue-eyed boys seemed to be in holiday mode and instead of criticising me he should have been on their case. One word led to another and before long we were tearing verbal lumps out of each other.

I don't think he has ever forgotten or forgiven what happened in Canada. From then on it seemed to me that he has borne a grudge. One incident in the wake of that tour annoys me to this day, simply because I thought he was being so petty. It was the day of Colin Jackson's testimonial match against Everton. I was of course keen to play. Bomber and I had played together in the heart of the Rangers – and Scotland – defence for years and I wanted to honour him for the great contribution he had made to the club. As it was a bit of a gala occasion I even brought Linda and my two daughters along.

However, much to my dismay, Greig didn't select me for the game. In fact I wasn't even on the bench. What made it worse was that he didn't have the decency to tell me himself and instead dispatched Joe Mason, the first-team coach, to give me the bad news. I wasn't injured so I could only come to one conclusion: John was still angry about what had happened in Canada and was unwilling to bury the hatchet.

While being left out of Bomber's testimonial was disappointing in my view it wasn't that important compared to how I was treated when I left Rangers at the end of season 1981/82. Due to a succession of serious knee injuries I had been advised to retire from football by a specialist. In recognition of my ten years of service, and given that my career was being cut short (I was thirty-three, not that old for a central defender) the club had agreed to pay me £10,000. Around the same time I was granted a testimonial, which was to be organised not by Rangers but by a voluntary committee, which would have meant me receiving two lump-sum payments.

But I never received the money from the club.

One day in his office John put it to me that as I would be getting the proceeds from the testimonial I wouldn't want the £10,000 from Rangers as well. Foolishly, I went along with his suggestion. I agreed not to take the club's cash and of course the money stayed in the Ibrox coffers.

Rangers would not have been out of pocket no matter what happened because I am pretty sure they had an insurance policy that covered them against players being forced out of the game through injury. So why couldn't they just have paid me the money?

I will never know the full facts and I am certainly not accusing anyone of acting in bad faith. It may be that the board, aware of the forthcoming testimonial, instructed John to make the suggestion to me. Another possibility, I believe, is that it could have been John's own idea and if that was the case I would be very disappointed because I played with, and under, him for so long. Even today I am angry about it, not only because of the money – although it would have come in handy at the time, given that I had a wife and a young family – but also because I feel that whoever was behind the decision I was taken advantage of.

It has left a bitter taste in my mouth.

19

Leaving Rangers

My last two seasons at Ibrox – 1980/81 and 1981/82 – were to say the least mixed. I was still troubled with my knee, which restricted my appearances and even when I was fit I often filled a new and unfamiliar role: on the bench as a substitute. We were also-rans in the league, finishing third twice but well behind Celtic and Aberdeen. I had been glad to see Willie Johnston rejoining the club (from Vancouver White-caps in August 1980) but not even his mercurial talents could inspire us.

It wasn't as if there hadn't been investment in the side. After keeping a tight rein on spending in the early part of Greig's tenure as manager the purse strings had been well and truly loosened. In fact one newspaper calculated that Rangers had spent almost £1 million over the previous two years with the likes of Stevens, Redford, McAdam, Bett, Johnston and latterly John McClelland arriving.

There were three problems. In the first place the squad wasn't as good as it had been in the Seventies. Many Rangers fans looked enviously at the guys playing for our main rivals. Aberdeen had, among others, Leighton, Miller, McLeish and Strachan while Celtic, in addition to home-grown talents like Burns, McGrain, Aitken and Nicholas, had purchased wisely during their forays into the transfer market. As well as buying Frank McGarvey from Liverpool manager Billy McNeill had snapped up two guys who had been boyhood Rangers fans: Davie Provan and Murdo MacLeod; both I am sure would have been excellent signings for us. Our second problem was

John Greig's tactics. He tended to set out the team in a 4:4:2 formation, which meant there was rarely a starting place for our greatest talent, Davie Cooper. The third problem, which I have alluded to elsewhere in this book, was John's lack of man-management skills.

Although on the big occasion we could still turn it on we were dreadfully inconsistent, especially away from home, where our record was very poor. While we matched or even bettered Celtic and Aberdeen in terms of home form we were dismal when we didn't have the comfort blanket of Ibrox. In fact during the two seasons I am talking about we won only ten away games, compared to twenty-six for Celtic and nineteen for Aberdeen. That is perplexing given that ground reconstruction was under way on the stadium, which lent it a strange atmosphere when only three sides were in operation.

To my mind there is a game that summed up our league form in those seasons. It was an Old Firm encounter at Ibrox in April 1981. I was out injured and my place in the centre of defence was taken by Derek Johnstone. That meant we had to go with Ian Redford and Colin McAdam as our strike force. To be honest they didn't get a kick, despite their expensive price tags. It wasn't just them. Jim Bett, another of the big buys, had a poor game and was substituted. Celtic won 1–0 virtually sealing the title in the process. But the narrow score-line flat-tered us. We rarely troubled them and I don't recall ever seeing us so toothless in an Old Firm game, especially at home.

If those two league campaigns were grim our record in the cup competitions was a little better. Better that is if you overlook the debacle that was Chesterfield.

We hadn't qualified for Europe in 1980/81 and had entered the late and unlamented Anglo Scottish Cup, which in terms of prestige is probably up there with the Johnstone Paint trophy. After knocking out Partick Thistle in the first round we were paired with Chesterfield of the English third division in the quarter-final. The first leg was at home and it was a game that on paper we should have won comfort-ably. But we huffed and we puffed and eventually trooped off the pitch with a 1–1 draw and a chorus of boos ringing in our ears.

If that was bad what happened in the return was catastrophic. In front of their biggest crowd in many a year – which included three thousand travelling Rangers fans – little Chesterfield played us off the park, scoring three fine goals without reply to make the final aggregate score 4–1. To make matters worse their two-goal hero, Phil Bonnyman, had once been a Rangers player but was given a free transfer after playing only one first-team game. I played in both legs of a tie that the *Glasgow Herald* called the biggest humiliation for Rangers since Berwick. I agree with that analysis; a result like that is simply unacceptable for a club like Rangers.

The only consolation was that we demolished Celtic by three goals to nil in our next game. It was probably the best fixture we could have had after the shambles of Chesterfield. We knew that if we could win an Old Firm game the fans might be prepared to forgive and in time forget. The only disappointment for me was that I was an unused substitute for the Celtic game as Greig went back to the partnership of Colin Jackson and Derek Johnstone in central defence.

The League Cup was also a big disappointment. In 1980/81 we were eliminated in an early round by Aberdeen and the following season I played in most of the games on the road to Hampden, only to miss out on a place in the team for the final, a game that Rangers won 2–1.

However, I did yet again taste success in the Scottish Cup, winning my ninth and last major honour with Rangers. We put in some decent performances, including a 5–0 demolition of Airdrie and a 3–1 defeat of Hibs in the quarter final. Then we were off to Celtic Park for the semi, where we faced a Morton side whose inspiration was the so-called Idle Idol, Andy Ritchie.[35] To be quite honest it was a kicking match from start to finish, with referee Brian McGinlay sending off Jim Holmes and Bobby Thomson of Morton and booking eight others, including me. McGinlay even had to stop the game at one point in order to speak to the two captains about the mayhem. But we survived, despite a Morton penalty converted by Ritchie, thanks to goals from Bomber and Bobby Russell.

---

[35] Andy was a fine talent with bags of technical ability. He was particularly adept with the dead ball and scored many goals from free kicks. He was voted player of the year in 1979 by the football writers while with Morton, a rare accolade for someone turning out for a small provincial club.

In the final we were up against Jim McLean's Dundee United, a team packed with top-class players like Paul Sturrock, David Narey, Paul Hegarty and Hamish McAlpine. It turned out to be a scrappy – and goalless – affair with the men from the east by far the better side. I didn't play that well and was deservedly booked for a foul on Sturrock.

The pundits fully expected United to prevail in the replay but John, for once, decided to throw caution to the wind. He sent out an attacking side that included Davie Cooper (a substitute in the first game) and Derek Johnstone (injured for the first game) in the starting eleven.

The result was pure magic.

We tore Dundee United apart with fast, attacking football, running out 4–1 winners thanks to a brace from John McDonald and one each from Messrs Cooper and Russell. It was a great way to lift our first trophy for two years. Of course I had no way of knowing it would be the last silverware I would ever win at Ibrox.

By the time 1981/82 came around I was on borrowed time as a Rangers player. I actually played in the first dozen league games and in seven cup ties but my last game in light blue was on 14 November 1981, a 4–1 win over St Mirren at Ibrox.

It wasn't as if I couldn't compete. As late as 1 November 1981 Allan Herron wrote a glowing profile in the *Sunday Mail* in which he argues that 'There is a very good reason why Rangers have reached the final of the Scottish League Cup on 28 November – Tom Forsyth. He has been the crutch of every player around him. The inspiration of his co-defenders. The loud rebuke when forwards lose their way.'

To those looking in from the outside there was something in what he said. But it didn't feel that way to me. You will know that Biblical expression, 'The spirit is willing but the flesh is weak.' That was me. With fifteen years experience in the professional game I could read the game better than at any time in my career but increasingly I couldn't get there in time to make the tackle or the interception. I had already had two major operations on my knee, a problem that was further compounded when someone fell over on it during a training session.

I will always remember the consultation with the specialist. He confirmed that I would do the knee even more damage if I kept on playing. Disappointed though I was I knew that I had to give up the game I loved. An announcement was made in March 1982 that I had been forced to quit on medical grounds at the age of just thirty-three, an age when many central defenders are at their peak.

20

My Rangers Dream Team

It took me all of two minutes to come up with this team, which is testament I suppose to the incredible consistency of the players over a long period. Later in this book I select my Motherwell dream team, an altogether harder task that took me several hours to complete, and even then I still had some reservations. But the Rangers guys picked themselves; there is no debate because each and every one of them was exceptional.

In a classic 4:4:1:1 formation I go for this eleven.

Peter McCloy
I had the good fortune to play with big Peter at Motherwell and followed him to Ibrox. We have always been great friends but that is not why I have picked him for my team. In my humble opinion the club's longest-serving keeper was a top-class operator with all the natural advantages that a six-foot-four frame gives you. He was also a tremendous shot-stopper, an excellent organiser and then there was his secret weapon: his prodigious kicks from hands, which set up many chances for our strikers. He had great success at Ibrox, including of course being a member of the team that lifted the European Cup Winners Cup in 1972.

Sandy Jardine

To me Sandy was a world-class player, someone who could hold his own in any company as he showed with his displays for Scotland and in two European finals with Rangers. He had all the attributes that a modern-day right back needs and then some. He was quick, stylish, elegant and equally strong in defence or on the overlap. An excellent trainer he was always super fit, enabling him to play for more than two decades in top-class football. He was rightly named player of the year in 1975 and then, astonishingly, in his late thirties, was given the same accolade in 1986 while with Hearts, the only player to achieve this feat with different clubs. He seemed to be an ever-present and the only time I remember him getting injured was when he fell over an orange ball when we were playing Stirling Albion at Ibrox. More importantly, he is a really nice guy.

Colin Jackson

I played the best football of my career alongside Bomber. He was an excellent all-round centre half and an incredibly powerful header of the ball. I can vouch for how good he was in the air because in a League Cup final he accidentally headed the back of my head, knocking me for six. It says everything about how strong Scotland were in the 1970s that he won only eight caps. The only problem I had with big Colin was his thick Aberdonian accent: although he was born in London he spent his formative years in the Granite City, which made communication difficult in our early years together!

Dave Smith

If I can't select myself I would go for Dave, who was a very cultured player with a sweet left foot. Equally comfortable on the left side of midfield he was also brilliant as a football-playing centre back, someone who could effortlessly build moves from defensive positions. Another member of the team that won the European Cup Winners Cup in 1972, when he was also voted Scotland's player of the year by the football writers.

Willie Mathieson

Willie 'Wan Fit' Mathieson may have, as his nickname indicates, used his right foot only for standing on but to me he was the archetypal unsung hero. He was a highly competent left back and the fact that he was picked by managers of the calibre of Scot Symon, Davie White, Willie Waddell and Jock Wallace shows the quality of the man.

Tommy McLean

Rangers have a proud tradition of producing great wingers – from the 'Wee Blue Devil' Alan Morton to Willie Waddell and Willie Henderson – but to me Tommy McLean is up there with the best of them. If you had to compare him to a modern-day player it would be David Beckham because both men were immaculate in the art of accurate distribution. I don't think I have played with or against someone who could cross the ball, from any part of the pitch, with such unerring accuracy. He was immensely productive, a result I think of the arc of his crosses, which seemed to go much higher than those of any other player, making them very hard to defend. He had innumerable assists, helping the likes of Derek Johnstone and Derek Parlane rack up the goals. He was also a deep thinker about the game, which became even more apparent to me when I was his assistant in our time in management at Morton and Motherwell.

John Greig

There is nothing much I can say about this man that hasn't already been said. He was not only a great player and a great captain but also with his indomitable, never-say-die attitude he was someone who came to epitomise the spirit and traditions of this wonderful club, like Davie Meiklejohn in the 1920s and George Young in the 1950s. He richly deserves his accolade as the greatest-ever Ranger. When I was at Motherwell I admired him tremendously and I never dreamt I would get the chance to play alongside him at Rangers. He helped me a lot when I arrived at Ibrox and I will always be grateful to him for that.

Alex MacDonald

Wee Doddy was undoubtedly the most underrated player I ever took the field with and I am sure any of my former teammates would say the same thing. His work rate and commitment were both exceptional and the way he got up and down that park for ninety minutes was testament to his fitness. He also had the habit of chipping in with vital goals in big games, which to me made him the complete midfielder. Let's put it this way: I would rather have him in my team than see him lining up for the opposition. Born and raised in Glasgow he is probably the most Rangers-minded of my picks, something that clearly shone through every time he pulled on that light-blue jersey.

Derek Johnstone

Thanks to his extraordinary timing and powerful physique Derek was the best header of a ball I have ever come across. DJ was a phenomenal goal-scorer, which made his wish to play at centre half all the more baffling. To me he was never a defender – as the saying goes he couldn't mark a blackboard. I just think he was lazy by nature: when you play up front it is much more demanding, both physically and mentally and he didn't always come across to me as being up for that challenge. I also thought his attitude in training left a lot to be desired. That said he was an exceptional striker for Rangers. I also believe that he should have been used more by Scotland, especially in the 1978 World Cup but Ally was determined to stick with his tried-and-trusted strike force of Jordan and Dalglish. I remember one game against Wales when he bulleted a header into the back of the net. I will never forget the speed of that header; it was faster than most strikers could manage with their feet.

Davie Cooper

People today rave about guys like Lionel Messi and Cristiano Ronaldo. Rightly so. They are wonderful players. But for sheer skill they couldn't touch Davie Cooper. He had a love affair with the ball, and would protect it as if his life depended on it. I know only too well how good he was because, much to my disgust, he nutmegged me every day at training. Allied to his excellent passing, dribbling and crossing he had a ferocious shot, especially from free kicks, and he also took a mean penalty.

Willie Johnston

'Bud' had exceptional pace and, in fact, over five yards he was greased lightning. For a winger he was also a prolific scorer, scoring 126 times for Rangers, including of course two of the goals in the 1972 European Cup Winners Cup final. In my team I would play him up front supporting Derek Johnstone with Coop just in behind those two. That would have been some strike force. Bud's only problem was his temperament, which saw him get into trouble with referees more times than he will care to remember. He is also still in trouble with Tam Forsyth on account of the number of fags he cadged from me over the years!

Manager: Jock Wallace

The best manager I ever had the privilege of playing under and someone who did an enormous amount for my career. He was enthusiastic, dedicated and someone who gloried in being part of what he saw as the greatest club in the world. You always dreaded meeting him in the corridor at Ibrox and the first time I did he punched me playfully in the stomach and asked: 'What's it like to be a Ranger?' He meant to deliver a playful punch but not knowing his own strength the big man winded me. After that I gave him a wide berth! I also appreciated the way Jock would back you in the press and with officialdom when the going got tough. He was loyal to his players, something that we greatly appreciated.

Jock could also take a joke, despite his apparent gruff demeanour. There is no better example of that than the weekend we went to a hotel in Dunkeld for a break. We had played a hard game on the Saturday and had another tough one in midweek and Jock felt that a little time away would do us the world of good. He let us go out for a pint on the Saturday night and when we were in the pub a plot was hatched to play a practical joke on our manager. The boys had got into a conversation with two local police officers and saw their chance. They persuaded the cops to take Martin Henderson back to the hotel in a police car and when they got there the two boys in blue marched Martin up the front steps at the front door of the hotel. Watching this little scene unfold was one Jock Wallace, who was at the top of the stairs. He couldn't believe it. He had let us out for a few beers and one of us had behaved so badly that he had been arrested. There was steam coming out of his ears.

'What's going on here?'

'Martin got lifted boss,' one of the boys replied.

'You stupid bastard,' our manager raged as he surged down the stairs.

Jock was so angry that he tried to chin Martin, and would have connected had not the two cops held him back. I can still see the big man's face to this day. He had no idea it was a stunt and had completely lost the plot.

It was one of the funniest things I have ever seen and when Jock found out it was all a joke he had a right good laugh about it too.

21

Into Management and a Return to Fir Park

In September 1982 I was appointed manager of Dunfermline to replace Pat Stanton, who had moved on to manage Hibs, the team he had given such good service to as a player. I was thirty-three, but it was not just my tender years that led some to question the appointment. I had never even coached before, much less managed. I was able to add a bit of experience to the backroom by recruiting Cammy Murray as my assistant manager. I had played with him for a year at Motherwell before he became coach of the reserve side and I knew he was someone I could rely on. The Pars could certainly not be considered minnows; they were, and still are, a relatively big club, at least by Scottish standards.

Dunfermline were then in the first division, which had fourteen teams. The first division was the middle league in a structure that encompassed a premier league (of ten teams) and a second division, which also had fourteen teams. Dunfermline had been out of the top flight of Scottish football since the inaugural season of the premier league in 1975/76. After the glory years of the 1960s – when, with Jock Stein as manager, the club not only took part in two Scottish Cup finals, winning one, but also reached the semi-final of the European Cup Winners Cup – that was a real blow to their pride. However, the plain truth was that the club was in long-term decline. Most of the playing staff were part-timers and the quality was simply not there. When I took over from Pat we were in the bottom three and with no money to bring in new blood I was only too aware it would be a hard slog. In fact I was on a hiding to nothing but I took the job because I was desperate to stay in the game in some capacity.

However, I have to be honest and question whether my mindset was right. The disappointment felt after leaving Rangers had still not dissipated as Jim Traynor (then a young and aspiring journalist but now one of the great panjandrums of the Scottish media as sports editor of the *Daily Record* and a presenter on BBC Radio Scotland) discovered when he came to interview me at East End Park in November 1982.

In his article Traynor notes how modest and homely my little office was, observing that my chair had a broken arm, which I was 'rather sheepishly holding'. Ibrox, Traynor is implying, this most certainly was not. He clearly thought that both my heart and my mind were still in Govan, a notion that I did little to disabuse him of if this extract from his piece in the *Glasgow Herald* is anything to go by.

> [I watch him] shift uncomfortably in his chair in his office . . . it becomes apparent that the transition from player to manager is not going to come easily for Forsyth. Smoking almost constantly and flicking his lighter on and off, he points out that he was not ready to hang up his boots. His words are shrouded in regret.

Looking back I would like to say that my whole focus was on Dunfermline and on helping them to avoid relegation. The fact is however that leaving a club like Rangers, especially when the parting of the ways was due to injury, is incredibly hard. Perhaps subconsciously that affected my performance at East End Park. With the benefit of hindsight I also now appreciate how difficult it is to go straight from being a player into the manager's office.

We made a fight of it but the fact remains that we had some pretty poor results. I remember one game at home that we lost 4–0 to Partick Thistle, who were inspired by a brace of goals from their little ginger-haired striker. His name? Maurice Johnston. Then a week later we suffered another heavy home defeat, this time to Dumbarton who beat us three-nil, and to add insult to injury had two men sent off and were therefore left with only nine men on the park. After the turn of the year we managed to string together a few good performances and as a result took the fight right down to the last game of the season. Unfortunately, it was against champions St Johnstone. We lost 1–0 and were relegated, finishing a point from safety.

Inevitably, I got the sack and for the first time in sixteen years I was out of the professional game. I was fortunate; I got a second chance thanks to a good pal and former colleague.

In November 1983 Tommy McLean was appointed manager of Morton and he asked me to join him as his assistant manager. Morton were a part-time outfit playing in the first division but I jumped at the chance. To be honest I was delighted. Not only was it a chance to get back into football but also I would get the opportunity to work with a good friend. Tommy and I had always got on well, perhaps because we are both typical west of Scotland males: quiet, a bit dour but underneath real football men with a burning desire to succeed. Apart from those holidays in Arran we had shared a car when we went into training at Ibrox, which made sense because we only lived a few miles apart in what you might call 'Rangers country': me in Stonehouse and Tommy in Ashgill, a few miles from Larkhall.

In the fullness of time Tommy would prove himself to be a great manager but his abilities were obvious to anyone who came in contact with him. He was a deep thinker, an excellent tactician, a great man-manager, and, perhaps most important of all, he had a great eye for a player. These qualities were spotted by Jim Traynor, who had of course earlier been dispatched by the *Herald* to run the rule over me at Dunfermline. Traynor was clearly impressed by his meeting with Tommy, noting that he 'is too shrewd' to make rash statements about promotion as he realised 'they could come back to haunt you'. Instead, Traynor observes, Tommy would carefully assess the squad and the tactics before making any changes, which, Traynor argues, was a good, subtle, shrewd approach.[36]

---

[36] *Glasgow Herald*, 3 December 1983

And so it proved on the field of play. We won the first-division championship with a bit to spare and in so doing propelled Morton back to the big time. However, as so often happens, other clubs sat up and took notice. Motherwell had just been relegated from the premier league after a disastrous season under my old teammate, Bobby Watson, in which a mere fifteen points had been garnered. Bobby resigned and Motherwell began the search for a new management team.

Several candidates were considered but in the end Motherwell opted for Tommy, who asked me to go with him as his assistant manager. We had no hesitation in leaving Morton despite the fact that the Greenock outfit were going up to the premier league and Motherwell had been relegated to the first division. Motherwell were, always have been and still are a bigger club, a full-time club, a club with much greater potential. Motherwell were also a Lanarkshire club, a club that as local boys we had a lot of time for. It wasn't a hard decision.

There was clearly a major rebuilding job to be done at Fir Park. Money however was very tight and to free up funds one of our first acts was to sell two of our most experienced players in Stuart Rafferty and Kenny Black. Despite that we managed to steer our charges back to the premier league at the first time of asking, the second season in succession we had achieved that feat. We had won the title with Morton and repeated the feat with Motherwell, throwing in a great run to the semi-final of the Scottish Cup for good measure. We managed a draw against Celtic in the semi at Hampden but then lost by three goals to nil in the replay, still not bad for a lower-division club.

Those first few seasons back in the premier league were difficult. Financial restraints meant that we had to sell our best players. Ally Mauchlen and Gary McAllister were sold to Leicester City for a combined fee of £350,000 after just one league game had been played in season 1985/86, our first campaign after being promoted. Later that same season two more experienced guys, Andy Dornan and Graeme Forbes, also left to move down south. New guys were brought in but inevitably they weren't of the same calibre. The reduction in quality, allied to the constant chopping and changing, meant that we really struggled. We finished in ninth place, second bottom, and in any other year we would have been relegated. But we got a stroke of luck. The premier league was expanded to twelve teams and relegation was cancelled. It meant that the club would still be in the top tier of Scottish football for its centenary year of 1986/87.

The reprieve from relegation gave Tommy a bit of breathing space. Slowly but surely – and the process took several seasons – he began to build a squad that could compete at the highest level. Youngsters were blooded: Tom Boyd, Fraser Wishart, Jim Griffin, Chris McCart and Phil O'Donnell among them. More experienced guys arrived for modest fees or on free transfers, the likes of John Philliben, Stevie Kirk, Iain Ferguson and Dougie Arnott. Tommy also had a wonderful knack of bringing in top players who were at the veteran stage of their careers and squeezing a couple more seasons out of them; think here of Davie Cooper, Bobby Russell and Craig Paterson. It paid off. We were much more solid in the premier league and would never again be in relegation trouble during our time at the club.

We both realised that Motherwell would always be a selling club, another good example of that being Andy Walker who left for Celtic in 1987 for a fee of £375,000. All we could do was to bring in guys who would do us a turn and develop those already at the club. I think we did that. We constantly stressed to the players the virtues of hard work and application, of commitment, of acquiring good habits and sticking to them, just as Jock Wallace had done for us. We were also quite strict when it came to disciplinary matters because I think that being professional in all that you do goes to the heart of being a successful sportsman. If I can blow my own trumpet for a moment I think they became better players thanks to our tutelage.

When I wasn't coaching the first team I had many other duties, one of which was assessing young players who came to us on trial. They would arrive at Fir Park, aged fourteen or fifteen, and stay for a week or so, giving us the chance to assess them. Most were from Scotland's central belt, which meant they could get home to their families at night and then come back the next day after sleeping in their own beds.

One day, however, a young lad from Northern Ireland arrived. He was going to be with us for four days and given the distances involved the club had no option but to put him up in a hotel. He was a very quiet lad, probably away from home on his own for the first time, and at fourteen he was around the same age as my three children. If it had been one of mine I wouldn't have wanted them to stay in a hotel in a strange town on their own, so I said to Tommy:

'He can stay at my house for the time he's in Scotland. It will be company for him.'

'That's great Tom. I am sure the boy would really appreciate it,' our esteemed manager replied.

And that is how Neil Lennon, the future manager of Celtic, came to be a house guest of Tom Forsyth for four days.

I thought it would be nice for Neil to have the chance to see a game while he was in Scotland so I phoned Jocky Scott, the manager of Dundee – whose team happened to be in action while Neil was over – to get tickets for me, my son David and Neil. Yes, you've guessed it: Dundee were playing Rangers! Not only that, the tickets were for the area at Dens Park reserved for away fans so Neil ended up sitting amongst thousands of Rangers fans.

We didn't sign Neil. He was still very young and we decided instead carefully to monitor his progress. It turned out, however, that he later signed for a club down south. The other thing that sticks in my mind about Neil is the size of his feet. They were huge, which meant that, even at the age of fourteen, he wore size-twelve boots.

22

Motherwell 1991: the Family Final

I have been very fortunate in the Scottish Cup. I scored the winner in the centenary final, which just happened to be one of the greatest games ever seen at Hampden, and I was part of two treble-winning teams as well. Then, in 1991, I played my part again, this time as a member of the management team that helped Motherwell to its first triumph in the competition for thirty-nine years. That game in '91 with Dundee United, which of course became known as the 'family final', was also a magnificent spectacle, one of the most exciting ever to grace the old stadium. It also gave me the chance to parade a trophy to the fans from an open-top bus, something that because of the bitterness of Old Firm rivalry would be impossible to do in Glasgow.

I had a feeling we might do something that season. Tommy had well and truly made his mark on the side and we were now a match for anyone on our day, making us ideally suited to cup football. After solid performances in pre-season friendlies we started the season proper in fine style, beating Celtic 2–0 in our first league outing at Fir Park. From there we put in a solid campaign in the premier league, finishing sixth in a division of ten.

However, it was in the Scottish Cup that we really showed our mettle, despite getting one of the worst draws possible in the third round. It sent us to Pittodrie on 26 January 1991 to face an Aberdeen side still full of quality players, a side that would take Rangers to the last game of the season in the battle for the championship. The Dons finished two points behind the Ibrox men but a massive twelve points ahead of Celtic.

Aberdeen's class shone through right from kick-off. In fact they were all over us. After some sustained pressure early in the game we were more than a little fortunate when the linesman flagged for offside when big Alex McLeish forced the ball over the line. It was the same for most of the first half, with Aberdeen constantly on the attack. But a combination of missed chances and superb saves by our keeper, Ally Maxwell, kept the score-line goalless. I remember thinking that we had to come into the game at some point, and sure enough, thanks mainly to Davie Cooper's clever promptings in midfield, we did. With the game now more evenly balanced both teams fought hard for the opening goal, but with defences on top it looked more and more likely that a replay at our place was on the cards.

Then Tommy Mclean played his joker.

Tommy pulled off Iain Ferguson, who had put in a punishing shift up front, and replaced him with Stevie Kirk. It was an inspired substitution. Big Stevie got on the end of a perfectly executed free kick from Davie Cooper (who else?) and he fairly lashed a first-time shot past Theo Snelders in the Aberdeen goal. It was, to be fair, slightly against the run of play but we couldn't have cared less. Kirk's goal put us in the hat for the fourth round.

Next up were Falkirk, then one league below us in the first division but near the top and strong contenders to win promotion. The tie was at Fir Park and with the majority of the ten thousand-plus crowd behind us we got off to a real flier when Nick Cusack slotted home a cross from Davie Cooper. But fair play to Falkirk they fought hard and snatched an equaliser, which sent the teams in level at half-time. In the second half we took the lead for the second time, through Joe McLeod, before they once again levelled the tie. It was time for supersub Stevie Kirk to come to the rescue. He came off the bench to score our third and, late in the game, Cusack got his second to give us a deserved 4–2 win.

We were now in the quarter final and just ninety minutes from a place in the last four. We fancied our chances against anyone at Fir Park so we were well pleased when the draw paired us against Morton, another team from the first division. In truth, and despite our confidence, we played really poorly and I have to admit that Morton probably deserved to beat us. We were relieved to escape with a goalless draw and to go to Cappielow for the replay. Once again it was a hard-fought match. Tom Boyd scored a rare goal, although he didn't really know much about it because the ball hit him rather him hitting the ball. After that Morton pushed and pushed for the equaliser and, irony of ironies, it was scored by a former Motherwell player, one of the most popular players ever to have pulled on that famous claret-and-amber jersey.

Step forward John Gahagan.

John had left Motherwell at the end of season 1989/90 after giving ten years of sterling service to the club, service that was recognised by a testimonial match and a gala dinner. He was much loved by the crowd, not only for his often dazzling performances on the wing but also because he was a lifelong Motherwell fan. It was probably inevitable that he was going to score that night and sure enough he did. When Ally Maxwell failed to hold a fierce drive Gahagan pounced and rifled the ball into our net.

Despite the best efforts of both teams, which continued into thirty minutes of extra time, there was no further scoring. The semi-final berth would be decided by a penalty shoot-out. I was quietly confident we would prevail. We had a lot of big personalities in the side. As well as Davie Cooper and Bobby Russell, who had of course played in so many high-profile games at Rangers, our other penalty takers were: Iain Ferguson, who had joined us from Hearts and had also played for Dundee United in the 1987 UEFA Cup final; super-sub Stevie Kirk; and one Colin O'Neill, a Northern Irishman and one of the game's great characters, loved by our fans for his never-say-die attitude but hated by the opposition. I was right. Every one of our boys stuck away their penalty with aplomb and with Morton missing one of theirs we were through.

The four semi-finalists were Dundee United, St Johnstone, Celtic and of course Motherwell. Most clubs are desperate to avoid an Old

Firm club in the semis so we seemed to have drawn the short straw when Celtic's name was placed next to ours. But Tommy and I were quietly confident we could cause an upset. Celtic had some excellent players: McStay and Collins were the pick of the bunch but we weren't going to lose any sleep about facing the likes of Chris Morris, Anton Rogan, Gerry Creaney and Joe Miller.

There was a lot of controversy during the 2010 World Cup about FIFA using a new ball for the finals, one that had a much greater tendency to move in mid-flight. It was the same in the run-up to our semi-final in ninety-one. In their infinite wisdom the SFA, perhaps due to a change of sponsor, introduced a new, lighter ball. We got our hands on a supply of the new balls and I put on a training session to test them out. However, the players, as you do with a new ball, were hitting it far too hard, with most of their efforts ballooning over the bar. They needed to be less forceful because the new ball, being lighter, had a tendency to dip earlier as it flew through the air.

As time passed more and more of their shots were on target. Little did I know that their proficiency with the new ball would soon pay a huge dividend.

The semi-final with Celtic, on a wet and windy night at Hampden, was disappointing as a spectacle. On the other hand we were disappointed not to have won the game. Iain Ferguson struck the bar with a pile-driver and we were also denied a certain penalty so we left the national stadium that night harbouring a definite sense of injustice. There was also a slight sense of apprehension. After all, not many teams get a second chance against either Celtic or Rangers.

We needn't have worried. The eleven players we sent out in claret and amber for the replay turned in one of the greatest performances in the history of the club.

Motherwell: Maxwell, Nijholt, Boyd, O'Neill, Philliben, McCart, Arnott, Griffin, Ferguson, O'Donnell, Angus

It was a great blend of youth and experience. Tom Boyd was still a relatively young player while Chris McCart had broken through from the youth ranks in the previous two seasons. Phil O'Donnell, who would become such a fine player, was aged nineteen and had only just been signed from Motherwell Boys Club. Among the more experienced guys were Luc Nijholt, who we had signed from Old Boys of Basel for a club record fee of £100,000 at the start of the season, John Philliben, another Motherwell stalwart, and of course the tireless Dougie Arnott up front. Our only problem was that Davie Cooper, who would have relished the big-time atmosphere, was suspended and was working as a summariser for Sky Television.

At half-time I am sure all the journalists in the press box were writing exactly the same story: you only get one chance against the Old Firm. Celtic had taken the lead through a Tom Boyd own goal and although we equalised thanks to a fine shot from Dougie Arnott – with his left foot for a change – Rogan put them 2–1 ahead going into the break. Normal service had been resumed.

Or had it?

I remember that wee Tommy ripped into the guys at half time. He had to. If we repeated that first-half performance we would be dead and buried. It worked. The boys tore into them in that second half and I don't think Celtic knew what hit them. Not long after the restart Arnott got his second with a header that bulleted past Packie Bonner. The game was now level.

Then came the goal of the season.

In the sixty-ninth minute Colin O'Neill picked the ball up a full forty yards from goal and thundered a magnificent shot into the Celtic net. It was a stunner but I don't believe he would have managed it without the hard practice we had put in on the training ground with the new ball. Celtic were down and when Stevie Kirk scored his statutory goal-after-coming-off-the-bench in the eighty-fifth minute they were out for the count. Motherwell were in their first Scottish Cup final for four decades.

Talk about cup fever. I recalled the frenzy that accompanied our Texaco Cup games in the 1970s against Stoke and Tottenham. I could also remember the scramble for tickets when we faced Rangers in a Scottish Cup quarter final in 1972 at Fir Park, a game seen by an incredible crowd of 28,000. But the build-up to the 1991 final was something else again.

As soon as we beat Celtic the whole town went crazy. Shops decorated their windows in claret and amber, bank staff dressed up in

Motherwell strips while schools ran competitions to design good-luck cards for the team. The streets in the town centre were covered in bunting and posters and huge banners with 'Come on the Well' were hung from road signs and lamp-posts.

Then the scramble for tickets began. When the date of sale was made known to the Motherwell public, fans slept overnight in their cars just to be sure of a stand ticket. The queues that morning were unreal and it wasn't long before our initial allocation was sold out. It was a bank-holiday Monday but the SFA agreed to open up their offices to supply our hard-pressed office staff with more batches of tickets. I believe that nearly thirty thousand Motherwell fans attended the final, but even then many were disappointed.

The excitement was heightened by the fact that there would not be an Old Firm team in the final. We would be facing Dundee United. It meant that whole families would be going, enjoying a day out in a congenial, carnival atmosphere. The other factor was that United were of course managed by Tommy's older brother Jim. It was the first time that two brothers had managed Scottish Cup finalists since before the First World War. The papers couldn't resist it: noting that mum, dad and the kids would be going to Hampden, and that the teams would be managed by siblings, they christened the game the Family Final. Motherwell also needed a bit of cheering up. The town had been devastated by the decline of heavy industry in the 1980s, epitomised by the running down of the giant steelworks at Ravenscraig, which was then on its last legs and would in fact close its doors for good a year later. In our own small way we had done something to make the town feel good about itself.

The build up to the final was a busy, yet happy, time. The media, with column inches to fill every day, thought up new angles on the game. One day Willie McLean – the third McLean brother and himself a former player and manager – was wheeled out to do a piece in which he points out that he 'was the only McLean brother who couldn't lose in the cup final'. Willie also notes in his article how this remarkable football family was hewn from the Lanarkshire pit village of Ashgill. Although there were no facilities for football in the village Tom McLean senior – father of Jim, Willie and Tommy – would spend his spare time cutting down bushes and levelling the ground on a pit bing so that his three boys would have somewhere to kick a ball about. With determination like that you can see how the brothers McLean got where they did.

One paper, the *Daily Record*, really pushed the boat out, making contact with the seven survivors of the victorious Motherwell Scottish Cup-final team from 1952 – guys like Willie Kilmarnock and Andy Paton – and treating them to a slap-up lunch at Hampden. This was followed of course by the inevitable photo opportunity on the Hampden pitch, with the old-timers holding the Cup aloft.

The current crop of players also got their day in the sun. There was a lot of interest in Colin O'Neill, beloved of the Motherwell fans for his aggressive, all-action style in midfield. I remember the first time I saw him play. It was a reserve game at Shotts, which we had arranged as a trial before making a decision on whether to sign him. He was overweight and most definitely not match-fit but Tommy and I were both really impressed by the way he got stuck into the opposition. He was also a really bubbly character, someone who could get the dressing room going, a bit like my old mate Dixie Deans. It wasn't a hard decision. We signed him and never regretted it. We soon found another facet of his personality: he was hyper, turning up for home games an hour-and-a-quarter early because he just couldn't wait – then being sick ten minutes before kick-off because his stomach was churning. It must have worked for him because he did us a right turn.

The stage was well and truly set for a wonderful day out. Players, fans, directors and the media had helped to create a genuinely happy atmosphere, one I think that the whole of Scotland bought into.

Then we got some terrible news.

On 15 May 1991, just three days before the final, Tom McLean senior died at the age of seventy-eight. It was a shattering blow for his three sons, especially as two of them were about to contest a cup final in our national stadium. Tommy handled his father's death with great dignity, as I am sure Jim and Willie did too, and although there were calls in some quarters for the game to be postponed neither Tommy nor Jim would entertain such a suggestion. They felt they had a duty to the fans to ensure that the game went ahead and that is exactly what happened.

In front of a crowd of 52,475, the teams lined up as follows:

Motherwell: Maxwell, Nijholt, Boyd, Griffin, Paterson, McCart, Arnott, Angus, Ferguson, O'Donnell, Cooper

Dundee United: Main, Krivokapic, Van Der Hoorn, Malpas, Clark, Bowman, McKinnon, McInally, Jackson, French, Ferguson

I imagine most people, including the bookies, had United down as favourites. After all they finished higher up the league than us in 1990/91, as they had done in every season since our return to the premier league in 1985/86. They also had some very good players, including two that I would put in the excellent category: Duncan Ferguson and Maurice Malpas. There was also the small matter of their manager, Jim McLean, the man responsible for creating one half of the so-called New Firm of Dundee United and Aberdeen and without doubt one of the best managers this country has ever produced. So on paper at least they had the upper hand.

In the early exchanges that's how it looked like panning out. With their fluent passing style United had us on the back foot and in the course of the first ten minutes they had a goal chalked off for offside followed by an effort that rebounded from our post. Gradually, however, we got back into it. Playing in his eighteenth cup final, an astonishing achievement, Davie Cooper was everywhere, prompting and probing, and although it is not something he is known for, tracking back constantly when United had possession. He had many able assistants. Luc Nijholt, our club player of the year, was a rock in defence, as was Craig Paterson, while Phil O'Donnell impressed everyone with his amazing box-to-box runs in the midfield. But we had many heroes that day, not least Iain Ferguson who opened the scoring midway through the first half.

A 1–0 lead at half time was pleasing for everyone but we suffered a major setback early in the second half when Ally Maxwell went down in a crumpled heap following a barge from John Clark, who is built like a heavyweight boxer. It was a very heavy challenge, one that merited a booking, but the referee did nothing. The problem was that Ally had been seriously hurt in the exchange and was in agony for the rest of the game, so much so that, near to collapse, he was taken to the Victoria infirmary for tests on his spleen and stomach muscles after the final whistle. A few minutes later Dave Bowman tested him with a long-range shot that, in normal circumstances, Ally would have saved easily. Unfortunately, with the knock from Clark causing him real discomfort, he couldn't get across to the ball and it ended up in the back of our net.

That was the turning point. The boys had two choices: either let their heads go down or use what had happened to Ally as inspiration. I am pleased to say they chose the latter option. First Phil O'Donnell struck with a courageous header and then Ian Angus put us 3–1 in front with a fine shot from the edge of the box. Surely we couldn't lose it now.

Credit to Dundee United. They were undaunted and pulled one back through substitute John O'Neil but although they put us under real pressure they just couldn't break down a defence in which both big Craig Paterson and Luc Nijholt were outstanding. With the fans counting down the seconds until the final whistle the Cup was almost in our grasp. Then the unthinkable happened. In desperation they threw a cross into the box and Darren Jackson got his head to the ball before Ally Maxwell and the scores were level. The Scottish Cup of 1991 would be settled by extra time or possibly even by a penalty shoot-out.

The momentum was now very much with United and with a badly injured goalkeeper I feared the worst. It was once again time for Tommy to play his joker. He threw on Stevie Kirk at the start of extra time and the big man did what he had been doing in the Scottish Cup all season. He scored a vital goal, a great header at the back post. We managed to survive some real scares as the men from Tannadice pushed for an equaliser. I remember in particular a Malpas shot with just seconds remaining that Ally Maxwell somehow pushed over the bar. I have to pay tribute to Ally; it was courage above and beyond the call of duty to make that save given his injuries.

It meant that Tom Boyd, our captain, was able to walk up those famous Hampden stairs and lift the Scottish Cup. It also meant that for the first time in our history we would be playing in Europe. While Davie Cooper was picking up his fourth Scottish Cup winner's medal it was the first (and probably the last) medal for most of the boys. I was delighted for every one of them. They had worked incredibly hard to get there and had not been found wanting in the face of adversity. I was also delighted for our supporters, many of whom had struggled financially in the Eighties while others were worried about losing their jobs. One summed it up perfectly, telling the *Glasgow Herald* that 'it was the greatest gift the town could have been given bar a reprieve for Ravenscraig'. All in all not a bad afternoon's work.

In terms of the spectacle I think that both teams put on a wonderful game for the big crowd at Hampden and for the millions watching live on television. Indeed, the doyen of Scottish sports journalists, Mr Alex 'Candid' Cameron, said as much in the *Daily Record*, describing the final 'as one of the most fantastic this grand old stadium has ever hosted'. That wasn't much consolation for the men in tangerine jerseys, or for their esteemed manager. In fact some of their players were so aggrieved at the end of the game that they harangued the match officials about what they saw as dodgy decisions. One of them completely lost the plot, throwing a boot at referee David Syme. I understood how they felt. Putting so much work into a game that by any standards was an epic but getting no reward is a horrible feeling.

I will never forget the scenes as we paraded that famous old trophy: firstly on the Saturday after the match at Fir Park and then on the streets of Motherwell and Wishaw on the Sunday. Tens of thousands turned out to greet their heroes on the open-top double-decker bus. They were both great days, family days. I must mention the two unsung heroes: directors John Chapman and Bill Dickie. Both were real Motherwell supporters, Lanarkshire men, who had worked tirelessly in the club's interests. While they dealt brilliantly with commercial and off-the-field issues they were wise enough to take a back seat when it came to matters football. Tommy and I will always be grateful for that.

With the Scottish Cup in the bag, and European competition to look forward to, Tommy and I both felt that we had taken the club a long way from the dog days of the 1980s when we were happy just to be in the top division. But we were not content to rest on our laurels.

It was time to make a real challenge in the league.

23

Into Europe and a Championship Challenge

GKS Katowice of Poland was perhaps not the glamour tie Motherwell supporters had been looking for in the European Cup Winners Cup. It was after all the first time in the long history of the club that we had qualified for Europe. They would have been hoping for the likes of Roma, Atletico Madrid, Werder Bremen or one of the two representatives from south of the border, Tottenham Hotspur and Manchester United. But the fans enjoyed it all the same, with about five hundred of them making the long journey east for the first leg, which was played on 18 September 1991.

Despite not being one of the more illustrious names Tommy and I knew we were in for a hard shift. Katowice had qualified for European competition six years on the spin and were in the Cup Winners Cup thanks to a 1–0 win in the Polish cup final over Legia Warsaw, traditionally one of the country's leading clubs. Tommy watched then twice and despite their pedigree – and our poor league form in the run-up to the game in Poland – he felt that if we could get our strongest team out we had a real chance of progressing to the next round.

We flew out from Glasgow airport but this being Eastern Europe the journey was not without its farcical side. Our plane had to sit on the Glasgow runway for four-and-a-half hours while a demand by the authorities in Poland for an additional $10,000 in landing fees was

negotiated. The game itself I have to admit was a massive disappointment. They dominated from start to finish, winning by two goals to
nil, and the fact that our keeper Billy Thomson was named man of
the match tells its own story.

It didn't deter our fans from turning up for the second leg, which
was played two weeks later. More than ten thousand were at Fir Park
and we almost pulled off what would have been one of the greatest
results in our history. Stevie Kirk sent the crowd into raptures when
he opened the scoring after taking a pass from Davie Cooper. Sadly, it
wasn't to last. Katowice snatched an equaliser early in the second half,
which gave them a vital away goal and left us needing three more goals
to win the tie. The boys, despite that sickening blow, gave it their all.
Nick Cusack put us 2–1 ahead on the night after eighty-six minutes
and then Kirk got his second and our third in injury time. A brave
effort but it was just too little too late and we went out on the away-
goals rule.

In domestic competition our performances in seasons 1991/92 and
1992/93 were frankly disappointing. Our league finishes were tenth and
ninth respectively and we didn't exactly set the heather alight in the
cups either. That was disappointing given the expectations of our fans
after the Scottish Cup triumph. I think there were a couple of reasons
for our underperformance. In the first place our cup-winning team
would never play together again. Tom Boyd was transferred to
Chelsea while Craig Paterson, Ally Maxwell and Bobby Russell also
left for pastures new. The second reason was the Taylor Report and its
requirement that top-flight clubs should move towards all-seater stadia.
It meant that Fir Park had to be redeveloped and money that might
have been available to sign new players was diverted into infrastructure instead.

Tommy, in consequence, had to be even shrewder in the transfer
market and in how he brought on young players. He was successful
on both fronts. Paul Lambert, whose once-promising career at St Mirren
appeared to be stalling, was snapped up in 1993 while Tommy Coyne
was signed from Tranmere Rovers. Both made a massive impact at Fir
Park and would later distinguish themselves at the highest levels of
the game. Other solid professionals arrived: Rab Shannon came to us

from Dunfermline; Miodrag Krivokapic, once of Red Star Belgrade and a skilful defender, was a capture from Dundee United; Brian Martin was a buy from St Mirren. At the same time younger players were brought on, guys like Jamie Dolan, Rab McKinnon and Paul McGrillen. A new team had been built.

The result was that we came very close to winning the league title in 1993/94. Motherwell topped the league at several stages and the impressive thing is that we kept it going right to the business end of the season. For me the game that summed our season was at home to Rangers on Tuesday, 26 April 1994.

Motherwell: Dykstra, Shannon, McKinnon, Krivokapic, Martin, Philliben, Lambert, Dolan, Coyne, O'Donnell, McGrillen

Rangers: Maxwell, McCall, Robertson, Gough, McPherson, Pressley, Steven, Ian Ferguson, McCoist, Duncan Ferguson, Durie

We were on an impressive run of nine matches without losing but that paled into insignificance compared to the men from Ibrox, who had gone twenty-two without tasting defeat. It was end-to-end stuff right from kick off with both keepers busy throughout the ninety minutes. We struck first when John Philliben shot past Ally Maxwell and then had to endure wave after wave of attacks as Rangers pushed for the equaliser. Seb Dykstra was in top form and pulled off a string of magnificent saves before he was beaten in the twenty-seventh minute by a certain Ally McCoist. If anything that goal made us even more resolute and we once again began to dominate. The winning goal came just a minute before half-time. A brilliant move involving Coyne and O'Donnell set up Paul Lambert with a great scoring opportunity but just as he was about to pull the trigger he was unceremoniously bundled to the ground by Trevor Steven. Penalty, cried the home support. The referee agreed and Tommy Coyne coolly sent Maxwell the wrong way.

Those ninety minutes against Rangers showcased everything that was good about Motherwell that season: determination, spirit, a never-say-die attitude, not to mention some outstanding football. The two points we picked up put us five points behind them at the top of the league with three games to go. There was still an outside chance of us winning the league but the Old Firm very rarely slip up in these circumstances and so it proved. Mind you we didn't help ourselves, as we stumbled to a win, a draw and a defeat in those last three matches, a disappointing sequence that saw us finish in third, one point behind Aberdeen and four behind Rangers. However, in another first for the club, we had the satisfaction of qualifying for Europe through our league position.

We smashed one premier-league record after another that year. Third was of course our highest-ever finish and at the same time we beat our previous points record, which had been set in 1975/76. It was the same for goals scored and conceded and for games won and games lost: Motherwell had never done so well in any of these categories in previous campaigns in the premier league. We took pride in the fact that Tommy Coyne, after an outstanding season in claret and amber, became the first Motherwell player to feature in the World Cup finals when he was selected for the Republic of Ireland squad that travelled to the USA in the summer of 1994. A group of Motherwell players had also represented Scotland while we were at Fir Park, among them Tom Boyd, Phil O' Donnell, Davie Cooper and Chris McCart.

However, despite the excellence of our performances, in which our fans took great pleasure, things behind the scenes were far from harmonious. Tommy and I felt that after a decade or so of solid progress, and some outstanding achievements, we deserved better terms. But it wasn't just about our salaries. We were ambitious for the club and were looking for an increased budget for the playing staff to build on what had been achieved. Unfortunately, we could not reach agreement with the board and Tommy and I took the momentous decision to resign. We were then appointed manager and assistant manager at Hearts, which I have to say was not a happy time for either of us. Changes, big changes, were needed but we didn't get the time we needed to implement them and in fact we lasted just the one season at Tynecastle.

24

My Motherwell Dream Team

I reeled off my Rangers dream team in about ninety seconds. Those guys picked themselves. They were all so exceptional – a few were genuinely world class – you really couldn't have gone for anyone else. But for the 'Well it was different. I spent hours fiddling with formations, personnel and playing styles before I came up with an eleven I was happy with and even then I was still wondering if I made the right call. Maybe it's because I was at Fir Park in two completely different eras, making comparisons difficult. It's not that I didn't play with and manage some great talents while I was there. In fact when I think about it I was spoiled for choice; there were so many candidates that the whittling-down process gave me a real headache.

After much deliberation these are my men. Playing in a 4:4:1:1 formation, I think this eleven would have given any side in Britain a run for its money.

Peter McCloy
He is in my Rangers dream team, which I think speaks for itself, and his performances while at Motherwell were also top drawer.

Davie Whiteford
Davie came from a real football family. His brother John played for Hibs, his father turned out for several Scottish clubs and his cousin

Derek was also a pro with Airdrie. He was a stylish right back who was equally at home in defence and attack. Although he is in the club's hall of fame I feel he is something of an unsung hero, giving Motherwell great service for many years. Davie is now a leading light in the Motherwell former players association.

Tom Boyd

He started out on the lowest rung of the ladder as a YTS trainee but came on in leaps and bounds thanks to his dedication and determination, qualities he had by the barrow-load. I think he was also helped by the coaching skills and experience of manager Tommy McLean. Boyd had phenomenal running power, which made his best position full back, but he could also slot into a central defensive position when required (which is where I have selected him for this team). He was superb for us in the 1991 Scottish Cup final and it didn't surprise me when he later became captain of Celtic and was awarded seventy-odd caps for Scotland. A nice, quiet guy who deserved everything he got out of the game.

Willie McCallum

A local boy (from Coltness in Wishaw) Willie played at the end of the Ancell Babes era and was still at the club when I joined. He was always very good to me and helped me settle into the team after I made the step up from the Juniors. I thought he was an exceptional centre half: mobile, great in the air, a good distributor of the ball from defence. Another really nice guy and I was so sad when he passed away about three years ago.

Joe Wark

To me he will always be Mr Motherwell. He was absolutely dedicated to the club, on and off the park. His work rate and commitment on the pitch were frightening and I have never seen a player who won so many balls when the odds were 30:70 or even 20:80 against him. How he won some of those tackles defied the laws of physics, so much so that I nicknamed him 'Rubberlegs'. Before the game he always took his false teeth out and it must have scared wingers half to death when they saw this toothless banshee hurtling towards them. I am just surprised that he never won a cap for Scotland but that might have had something to with Messrs Jardine and McGrain.

John Gahagan

John was an orthodox right winger, a great dribbler who on his day could cut open any defence. He was also, unlike many wide men with the ability to beat a man, a great crosser of the ball. Perhaps surprisingly for such a flamboyant player he was a very shy and retiring type and as a coach you always had to be careful what you said to him in case he went into his shell. As a boyhood Motherwell fan he was unfortunate in that he left Fir Park for Morton the season we won the Scottish Cup after giving eleven years of outstanding service in claret and amber. In fact he scored a goal against us in the quarter-final at Cappielow that could have knocked us out. Despite that he took the time to send us a good-luck letter for the final, which was a really nice gesture. Nowadays he is a very successful after-dinner speaker, which, given his personality, is something that came as bit of a surprise.

Bobby Russell

He didn't get into my Rangers team but I am pleased that he made this eleven. Bobby was a technically gifted midfielder, with an exceptional touch and awareness. He was also one of the best passers of a ball that I have ever seen. With a bigger physique and the greater strength that goes with it you feel he could have been a world beater. A nice guy who was unfortunate to miss out on the 1991 Scottish Cup final due to injury.

Gary McAllister

I first saw Gary McAllister at Wrangholme, the place we used to go for training. The boys were playing four-a-side in a penalty-box possession game and both Tommy and I were awestruck by Gary's touch and technique. He also had great balance, a killer pass and an almost preternatural composure. In fact, in terms of natural ability I would rank him just behind Davie Cooper in the pantheon of players I have played alongside or coached. With Leicester, Leeds, Liverpool and, of course,

Scotland he showed he could mix it with the very best in the game. He is another great guy and, incidentally, a quite superb golfer.

Davie Cooper

What can I say about this man that hasn't already been said? Everyone at Motherwell – especially the younger lads – looked up to him for his skill and his achievements as a player. I will say it again. He was the best I ever shared a dressing room with, bar none. We were also delighted when he added to his tally of Scotland caps while at Fir Park.

Phil O'Donnell

I had gone with Motherwell's youth team to a tournament in France, a tournament in which Phil's commitment, work rate and running power were clear for all to see. When we got back I said to Tommy McLean that we had to sign him on full professional terms right away – before someone else did. Tommy didn't waste any time and in the years that followed Phil became a major asset to the club as a real box-to-box midfielder. He dovetailed brilliantly with Davie Cooper, who always instinctively knew when to release him with a well-judged pass. But he wasn't just a wonderful player, he was also a wonderful human being and that made his untimely death in 2007 at the age of just thirty-five all the sadder. I will never forget the day he died. I had just got home from a Rangers game and my son phoned to give me the terrible news. Such a great loss.

John 'Dixie' Deans

Everyone loved Dixie. He was such a great laugh on and off the park. A jovial character, he kept the dressing room going with his jokes and wisecracks. There are so many stories I could tell about him but, unfortunately, most of them are unprintable! However, I do remember one day after training we had all gone for lunch at Robb's, our favourite restaurant in Motherwell. After we had finished our meal I was driving along Motherwell high street and had stopped at the traffic lights. I heard a loud knock on the window. It was Dixie. I rolled down the window and when I did he stole my car keys. That was me well and truly stuffed: thanks to the bold Dixie I was marooned on a busy street with the drivers behind giving me dog's abuse for holding them up. When he wasn't kidding around he was one hell of a player. In the box he was instinctive, someone who invariably reacted quicker than the opposition. And when he did latch onto a chance nine times out of ten he finished it, simply because he was such a beautiful striker of the ball. Motherwell signed him for just £100 from Neilston Juniors, which must have been the steal of the century.

Manager: Tommy McLean

For me he had it all as a manager: great man-management skills; superb tactical insights; great at judging a player; a distinguished playing career, which always gives you a bit more credibility with players. But the training ground was where he laid the groundwork for what happened on the pitch. The sessions Tommy put on were always so meticulously planned, so well thought through. That was appreciated by the players, whose performances improved significantly. Don't just take my word for it. In his autobiography, Gary McAllister notes that '[Tommy McLean's] training was probably the best organised I have ever experienced because he knew exactly what he wanted to do every day and who he wanted to do it with. There was nothing haphazard about it and it was all pre-planned down to the finest detail.'[37] When you consider that Gary played for some of the biggest clubs in Britain that is high praise indeed. It wasn't just the win in the 1991 Scottish Cup final, but also the many impressive league campaigns. These culminated in third-place in 1993/94, when Motherwell finished just four points behind Rangers, and for long spells we even had a realistic chance of winning the title.

---

[37] *Captain's Log: The Gary McAllister Story* Gary McAllister with Graham Clark (Edinburgh 1995)

25

Working for a Living

I was well paid as a footballer but not well enough to retire from the world of work when I left Hearts in 1995. I had made a good living over the years but of course it was peanuts compared to the wages earned by today's crop of players. Nor did I have a pension scheme to fall back on. Today clubs ensure that players get access to good financial advice but making provision for the day you gave up football was unheard of in my day. So, away from the somewhat cloistered existence of the professional footballer, I was faced with the prospect of returning to the real world of work.

Although I enjoyed every minute of my time at Ibrox and Fir Park I wish now I had earned a bit more. All things being equal I would never have wanted to leave Rangers but if a Liverpool, a Manchester United or an Arsenal had come in for me, and the money was right, I would have gone down south. When you have three young kids sentiment, I am afraid, doesn't come into it. You have to do the best for your family. Although the football in England in those days was clearly not of the same standard as the turbo-charged Premiership of today it was still at a higher level than in Scotland so it would also have been a step up in professional terms.

I have no idea if English clubs did ask about me. The fact is we were never told. But I am sure there were enquiries. There must have been big clubs in England who would have bitten your hand off for players of the calibre of John Greig, Sandy Jardine, Alex MacDonald and

Derek Johnstone, to name but a few. Clubs then had the whip hand; they owned you. Freedom of contract was a concept that no one in football had even dreamt about and at the end of your contractual period you were expected to sign a new contract on the terms offered. If you refused to re-sign the club could effectively freeze you out of the game.

The only consolation for me as I returned to the nine-to-five world was that I was well used to working hard to put food on the table. All those years as a joiner on Lanarkshire building sites stood me in good stead; as well as toughening me up I also had a good trade to fall back on and in fact after leaving Dunfermline I had gone back to the tools for a few months. I also drew on my background, handed down from my father, in the field of market gardening. When I was assistant manager at Motherwell I ran a little business growing and selling plants. I live on a smallholding and at the time I had three big greenhouses, which, with the help of a couple of pals, I had built. So every morning before training, at about five, I would get up and begin work. In January and February I planted seeds, which, by May and June had grown into fine plants. Of course there was a lot more to it than that. One of the most time-consuming and intricate jobs is known as 'pricking' plants, which involves separating individual plants into boxes. People would come to the house to buy plants but the main outlet for the Forsyth market-garden enterprise was Linda's flower shop in Stonehouse. She sold our plants and also bought in flowers from the market, which she would arrange beautifully for her customers. Apart from football, gardening was without doubt my favourite job; it is in my genes. In fact I would still be doing it now had it not been for Mother Nature. One winter a gale, which was measured at one-hundred miles per hour, blew down the greenhouses, wiping out my little business in the process.

After that, I landed a sales job with the *Evening Times* and worked with the paper for two years. It was great. I got involved in sales and marketing, helping with promotions and the like. Then I joined the wholesaling arm of John Menzies, helping to deliver the morning papers to newsagents. That was a bit different again; it was a heavy, manual job and therefore very demanding physically. It also involved nightshifts, something that was completely new to me. But I thoroughly enjoyed the experience.

My next line of work was probably the most congenial. From about 2005 until 2007 I was the starter at Loch Lomond golf course. You won't get many better jobs than that: fresh air, beautiful scenery, involvement in a game I love, meeting nice people. I also ran into many famous faces. One afternoon Kevin Keegan – a man I had faced in Scotland–England clashes – was playing a round. He was told by the caddies that I was working there and, friendly as ever, he came over to my office for a chat. After I apologised for kicking him we soon got down to some serious reminiscing about the good old days and he remembered how, after scoring for England against Scotland at Wembley, he ran to the crowd behind the goals to celebrate. The problem was that Wembley had, as usual, been taken over by the Tartan Army.

'I went to celebrate my goal but all I got was thirty thousand V signs,' he grinned.

Kevin also told me a wonderful story that linked football, golf and his former manager at Liverpool, the legendary Bill Shankly, undisputed king of the one-liners. Shanks, apparently, didn't let his charges at Liverpool play golf, a policy that was most definitely not appreciated in the Liverpool dressing room. So, one day, Emlyn Hughes, the captain, and Kevin knocked on the manager's door.

'Emlyn wants a word with you, boss,' said Keegan.

'Well, what is it son?' growled Shankly.

'Can we play golf like Manchester United and Arsenal?' Hughes nervously stammered.

'Listen son. They can play golf. We will play football and win all the trophies.'

Nowadays I work for G. Hillan Masonry, a company based in Sandford, which is near Strathaven. I was grateful to the owner, Graham Hillan, for offering me the job and it is one I thoroughly enjoy. I am out and about all day, visiting sites, making sure the boys have the resources they need, checking that things are going according to plan. It is so much better than being cooped up in an office all day long. A lot of the Hillan guys, like Damien and Jason, are Celtic fans and there is always a lot of banter, good natured I might add, in the run-up to Old Firm games.

26

Football Today

I fear for Scottish football. At international level we are also-rans while our domestic game is rapidly going backwards. For a football-mad country that has produced some of the greatest players in history that is a sad state of affairs.

I am not one of those ex-players who takes the view that everything in my day was so much better. Let's face it I was on the receiving end of a few embarrassing defeats at the hands of foreign opposition. The difference is that we always seemed to have good, young players coming through. Just look at Scotland's record since our first foray into the World Cup in 1954. We have qualified for the World Cup finals on eight occasions while our club sides have won three European trophies – four if you count Aberdeen in the European Super Cup – and reached many semi-finals and finals. The problem is that the last time Scotland qualified for the latter stages of a tournament was in 1998 and our club sides have also started to slip after some good runs by the Old Firm.

I don't think we can make the excuse that we are bound to under-perform because we are a small country. After all Denmark, Slovenia, Switzerland and Greece qualified for the 2010 World Cup from the European zone. None of them are giants of the game and none of them have either our football traditions or our history.

Craig Levein, who is a very good manager, has a big job on his hands. He can't call on a Jardine, a Souness, a Dalglish or a Law. With all due respect to the guys he will be relying on in the European Championship qualifiers in 2010 and 2011 most of them would have never got anywhere a Scotland squad in the Seventies and Eighties. Like any patriotic Scot I am desperate for us to qualify for a major championship but, sadly, I think it is a long way off.

Why are we in such a mess? I think there are four main reasons. In the first place boys now have so many other things to occupy them. When I drive around Lanarkshire – without doubt a football hotspot – I very rarely see kids playing impromptu games of football. When I was their age I played morning, noon and night. If you don't get youngsters into the habit of playing at an early age they will never develop the skills needed to be successful.

The second reason is what I would call opportunity. There is very little organised football in our schools. The basic philosophy in our school system seems to be against the whole concept of competition in any area, never mind football. Pupils are not even encouraged to have a game in the playground, simply because of our modern-day obsession with health and safety. When I was a boy the school janitor or the PE teacher ran teams and we played every Saturday of the school year. We also played during every break and at lunchtime in the school playground. Allied to this is the lack of good facilities, something that was rightly highlighted in the *McLeish Report*.[38] We should have invested in the good years but, perhaps because of complacency, we didn't. Our climate is horrible and so we need all-weather facilities and indoor centres more than almost anyone else. Yet the provision we have made is wholly inadequate.

Thirdly, we don't make use of the wealth of experience we have in Scottish football. People like Jim McLean, Billy McNeill and John Greig should have a role, perhaps within the SFA. And why not use the

---

[38] A review of the way Scottish football is run and organised and set up by the Scottish Football Association in 2009. It was carried out by the former first minister of Scotland, Henry McLeish, himself a professional footballer in his youth.

many top-class former players we have as youth or community coaches? I just feel the SFA has done so little to develop the game in this country. I once applied for a job there myself and my application reached the desk of Jim Fleeting, who is part of the development and coaching operation although I am not sure what he does exactly. I didn't get the job but when the letter arrived it was addressed to my son, David, who was then aged ten! That to me is sadly typical of the way the SFA treats people. While I am on the subject of organisation why do we need three governing bodies in a country the size of Scotland? Surely the SFA, SPL and SFL could be merged. It would not only make for better, more streamlined decision making but also it would be a hell of a lot more economical.

Finally, other countries have got better. At one time Scotland would have considered a game against a Scandinavian country as a banker. No longer. Their international teams, amateur until the 1970s, have overtaken us. They spent the money on facilities and youth development and have reaped the rewards. Until very recently most of our leading clubs didn't even have their own training complexes.

I know from my own experience how bad things were. When I was at Motherwell as assistant manager in the mid 1980s and early 1990s our training venue was, as the saying goes, a moveable feast. We used any open area of grass we could get our hands on, including public parks and school pitches. It was a nightmare in the winter when all the outdoor areas were frozen. In the morning I would be on the phone to schools, community centres and council offices, doing my best to beg, steal or borrow indoor facilities.

One of our regular training spots was in Hamilton and every morning when we arrived at Fir Park we would attach a trailer to the team minibus and fill it with goals, balls, bibs and cones, before making the short journey across Lanarkshire. The training 'facility' in Hamilton was in fact just a large expanse of grass that people would use for everything from jogging to having a picnic and walking their dogs. It was the dogs that gave us the biggest headache, or should I say what they deposited on the grass during their walk. We never left Fir Park without a big shovel to clear up the dog shit! It sounds funny but we were doing our best to train and develop professional athletes. And if professional clubs had such poor facilities, what about our kids? Where were they meant to train and to develop their skills?

Things are better at Fir Park now. Motherwell has its own Astro-turf pitch and a designated training area but as with the rest of Scottish football progress has been glacial. Rangers showed the rest of Scottish football the way ahead with Murray Park, which is a magnificent facility, but more needs to be done, especially at grass-roots level. The opening of the indoor centre at Toryglen in Glasgow, next to Hampden, is a positive development but there needs to be somewhere like that in every town and city in the land, along with professional coaches to bring on our youngsters. It will cost money but this is our national game we are talking about.

* * *

What about Rangers? The club's financial problems and the search for fresh investment have been well documented. I hope we find a new owner quickly, someone with the resources needed to take the club back to its rightful place. I would not be in favour of community or fan ownership. It is a nice idea, and it seems to work well for the likes of Barcelona, but I don't think it is right for Rangers. We need a strong man at the helm, driving the club forward, able to take the right decisions without having endlessly to consult committees. Of course, at the same time, the club has to be open with the supporters, to let them know where we are going and how we intend to get there. Rangers fans deserve the best and I strongly believe that only someone with the right vision, and the power to make it a reality, is capable of delivering for them.

I dread to think how much worse things could have been if Walter Smith hadn't come back to Ibrox in 2007. He has done a wonderful job: taking the club not only to a European final but also to back-to-back titles at a time when our main rivals have had so much more money to spend is no mean achievement. But it is an uphill battle given that Rangers get a pittance from the broadcasters compared to clubs in the English Premiership and in other big European leagues.

To me the only realistic, long-term solution is for Rangers to leave

Scottish football. England would be my first choice. I know the Premiership recently voted unanimously against opening up their league to the Old Firm but that could change. In football, money talks and if Sky took the view that their product needed to be refreshed and renewed the whole thing might just open up. I would even urge Rangers to start off one league down in the Championship, provided they got a guarantee of a Premiership place if they finished in the promotion places. I am sure that after a short period of adjustment we would do well in the Premiership. It would be a virtuous circle: with increased revenues we could sign the best players and that would bring success and therefore even higher revenues.

I would even consider the so-called Atlantic League. Big clubs in small countries now have no chance of competing with teams from England, Spain, Italy and Germany. It means that the only thing major clubs like Benfica, Ajax, Anderlecht, Rangers and Celtic, all genuine giants of the game, can look forward to is an occasional run in the Europa League. That to me is nonsensical. Until things change the Champions League will be a four-country monopoly with clubs from smaller leagues completely excluded. Surely Rangers versus Benfica or Rangers versus Ajax would be more attractive to fans, and to the television companies, than Rangers versus St Johnstone or Rangers versus Kilmarnock.

The Old Firm going to pastures new would of course have a massive effect on the rest of Scottish football. It would diminish the top league, no doubt about it. The consolation would be that other clubs could actually conceive of winning the title: Hibs, Hearts, Aberdeen, Dundee United – even my old team, Motherwell. Talking of the 'Well, I am pleased to see them in such good health. After the horrors of administration they seem to be a much better-run club these days. I was so happy for Craig Brown and Archie Knox when they qualified for the 2010/11 Europa League. I can't see them winning the title under the current set-up but I would be on Cloud Nine if they managed to lift one of the cups.

In the meantime Rangers will just have to make the best of Scottish football. The way forward has to be youth development, indeed given the lack of money there is really no alternative. I think more could be done to help young players develop. A higher proportion of Murray Park youngsters should go out on loan deals to smaller Scottish clubs, not only to give them experience but also to toughen them up. And why not put Old Firm second strings in the lower leagues, but not allow them promotion, and fill them with promising youngsters. It is something I have been banging on about for years. It would be a massive boost for the boys to play against hardened pros and the clubs in the other divisions would benefit from increased gate money.

Another change I would like to see is the expansion of the Scottish Premier League to sixteen teams. Clubs meeting each other four times a season in the league – with the cup competitions making it possible for them to face each other five, six or even seven times – is a nonsense. It would also help the bigger clubs in the first division, the likes of Dunfermline, Dundee and now of course Falkirk, who struggle to pay for a full-time set-up on lower-league revenues. For the record I am not in favour of summer football. It is superficially attractive but people go on holiday in June and July while many fans like to get out for a game of golf or bowls.

My final thought has to be about referees. How could I leave out that fine, upstanding band of men (yes I am being a little sarcastic!). It is not so much the decisions they take – and I have suffered as much as anyone at their hands – it is the fact that they are not allowed to explain them after a game. Let them speak, openly and honestly, and not just through Hugh Dallas and the other referee supervisors. In fact I think it should be compulsory: after the media have interviewed the managers get the referees on for a chat. I am sure the fans – who after all are the people who bankroll our game – would appreciate being kept in the loop.

27

The View from Stonehouse

I count my blessings every day. I live in a nice house in Stonehouse, the town I have called home for nearly sixty years. Linda and I are so pleased that our three children Karen, Julie and David and five grandchildren live either in, or very close to, Stonehouse. The furthest-away member of our family, David, is in Strathaven just a few miles down the road.

I love spending time with my grandkids: Sophie, Mason, Emma, Cameron and Max. I am devoted to them. You might say that the so-called Iron Man of football is a big softie at heart, at least when it comes to his grandchildren. And don't they know it! I always give in to them; they can wrap me round their little finger.

I didn't make much money from football but none of us did in those days. But I can always fall back on my memories. I played for the team I supported, Rangers, more than three hundred times, and for my local sides: Stonehouse Violet and Motherwell, both of which I have great affection for. Then of course there is Scotland. No one could have been prouder than Tom Forsyth to pull on that dark-blue jersey. It meant so much to me then and it still does. I was also lucky in that some of my opponents on the football field were not only world class but also among the greatest of all time. Johann Cruyff,

Zico, Roberto Rivellino, Teofilo Cubillas, Mario Kempes, Johan Neeskens, Dino Zoff, Gordon Banks, Bobby Moore, Sir Geoff Hurst, Kevin Keegan, George Best, Kenny Dalglish, Jimmy Johnstone.

That is some list.

On the whole I believe that my career was a successful one. I won nine major trophies with Rangers, including two trebles. On the international front I won back-to-back home-international championships, beating England in both tournaments, while I was part of the side that eliminated the European champions in the qualifiers for the 1978 World Cup. With the right preparation we might even have done something special when we got to Argentina. On the managerial front Tommy McLean and I did some good work at Morton and Motherwell, although my spells at both Dunfermline and Hearts were both disappointing for different reasons.

I am honoured that Rangers have seen fit to recognise my contribution by inducting me into the Ibrox hall of fame. To be thought of in that way is immensely gratifying. Perhaps more importantly I have always enjoyed a great relationship with the Rangers fans. I meet many of them in my capacity as a match-day host at Ibrox and people still to this day ask for my autograph, although it is a bit disconcerting when they say 'My granddad used to watch you.'

I am always delighted to attend supporters' functions. In 2007, along with Sandy Jardine, Andy Goram, Ian Durrant and Davie Wilson, I was invited to the North American Rangers Supporters Association convention in Naples, Florida. I was surprised by the sheer number of Rangers fans who were there, at least three thousand I would guess, and they really did us proud. Nothing was too much trouble. Their passion for the club was clear for all to see as it is for Rangers fans all over the world and I wasn't in the least bit surprised when we took two hundred thousand to Manchester in 2008 for the UEFA Cup final.

I also take a keen interest in Motherwell. I am in the former-players club, which was started by Willie McSeveney and Davie Whiteford. Willie was the reserve-team coach when I was there and I played alongside Davie. We go to four home games a season and before the match we have lunch in the Vice-President's club. As you can imagine the good old days is always on the agenda and I swear if we go over that Texaco Cup semi-final with Hearts one more time we will succeed in rewriting history with Motherwell advancing to the final and not the Jambos!

I am able to catch up with some great characters at the FP club. Prominent among their number is Kirkie Lawson, who, forty years after we played alongside him in claret and amber, still regales his old comrades with the same corny jokes. To get my own back I remind about the time I left him speechless and, believe me, that takes some doing. What happened was that we were running round the track at Fir Park this day and as per usual Kirkie (who was a really good striker) wanted to know what I thought of his performance on the Saturday.

'How do you think I did on Saturday, Tam?'

'Aye you were all right Kirkie,' I replied.

A lap further on he asked again.

'How do you think I did Tam? Be honest.'

'Aye you were fine Kirkie.'

It happened on the next lap too. Same question, same answer. But when he asked for a fourth time I just had to shut him up.

'You were shite Kirkie.'

Cue one gobsmacked centre forward.

I was also delighted that my first club, Stonehouse Violet, will be up and running again in season 2010/11. The V-I-O have gone bust a few times but thanks to the efforts of many dedicated folk in the town we will be back in our rightful place in the Juniors once more. The team has a great history, including reaching the final of the Scottish Junior Cup in 1978, where unfortunately they narrowly lost (1–0) to Bonnyrigg Rose. I was unable to attend that match due to a pressing engagement elsewhere: the World Cup finals in Argentina. The only good thing about getting home from Argentina early was that I was able to take my place with the Violet's cup-final squad in the float for Stonehouse gala day. I will always be proud to have been the youngest player ever to represent the team. I should also say how proud I was to be asked to become honorary life president of the Violet, an invitation I was delighted to accept.

I am a regular on the golf course, often in the company of the guys I played football with and against. One of my regular partners is Cammy Murray, who was with me at Motherwell and Dunfermline, and he is some man when it comes to the golf! I remember one time we had arranged a foursome at Strathaven golf club: me and his son against Cammy and my son. It was a beautiful day and the course was very busy. As Cammy was teeing off he actually hit the metal box that is used for litter and when the ball flew vertically into the air he was able to catch it. The crash when the ball struck the box was so loud that everyone around the first tee ducked as they didn't have a clue where the ball was going. Cammy's other golfing mishap, which fortunately I didn't witness, was at the Kames Valley course. He sliced the ball so badly off the tee that it went straight through the windscreen of a passing car! He ran over to check that the driver was all right and to offer his apologies but as he told me later: 'It wasn't the right time to ask for my ball back.'

While I am a keen golfer, bowling is my main hobby these days. I play regularly at Stonehouse bowling club, as I have done for more years than I care to remember. I still have that old competitive urge although these days I don't win as many games as I used to. We are lucky to have had so many active members over the years and when new members have joined it has given the club fresh impetus and energy. Stonehouse has some fine bowlers: the McLeishs, the Robert-sons, Tom Notman and Hugh Smith to name but a few. It is a well-run and well-organised club, a real asset for Stonehouse.

The pinnacle of my bowling career came in 1996 when our club rink (Jim Wallace, Hugh Smith, 'skip' Jim Robertson and me) qualified for the Scottish championships at Northfield in Ayr. We managed to win our first-round match but then lost by a 'measure' in the second round. Despite that defeat it was a great experience for all four of us, the football equivalent of the Scottish Cup final and, let me assure you, just as disappointing to lose.

I must also mention the bowling club's infamous shadow committee, which is made up of Jack Ritchie, Drew Davidson, Ian Murray, Michael Philbin and Bill Brown. They won't go on the committee proper but they are quick to let the members know how things should be done, in the nicest possible way of course! They are a great bunch of lads and they certainly keep the committee members on their toes.

Touchwood I am still in good health, apart of course from my gammy right knee. It will never be right but I have learned to live with it. Bad knee or no bad knee I have no regrets about my football career. I have taken part in many historic games and played with, and against, some truly great players. It was an honour to share a football pitch with them.

I hope you have enjoyed reading about my career in football and about my life off the pitch.

Honours won

Club football

With Motherwell (as a player)
1968/69   Second-division winners

With Rangers (as a player)
1972/73   Scottish Cup
1974/75   League championship
1975/76   League Cup
           League championship
           Scottish Cup
1977/78   League Cup
           League championship
           Scottish Cup
1980/81   Scottish Cup

With Morton (as assistant manager)
1983/84   First-division winners

With Motherwell (as assistant manager)
1984/85   First-division winners
1990/91   Scottish Cup

Representative games

Scotland Under-23 v England 1971

Scottish League v English League 1971

Full caps (22)		**Honours**	
1971	Denmark	1976	Home-international
1973	Czechoslovakia		championship
1976	Switzerland (c)	1977	Home-international
	Northern Ireland		championship
	Wales		
	England		
1977	Finland		
	Sweden		
	Wales		
	Northern Ireland		
	England		
	Chile		
	Argentina		
	Brazil		
	Czechoslovakia		
	Wales		
1978	Northern Ireland		
	Wales		
	England		
	Peru		
	Iran		
	Holland		